Fish Talking

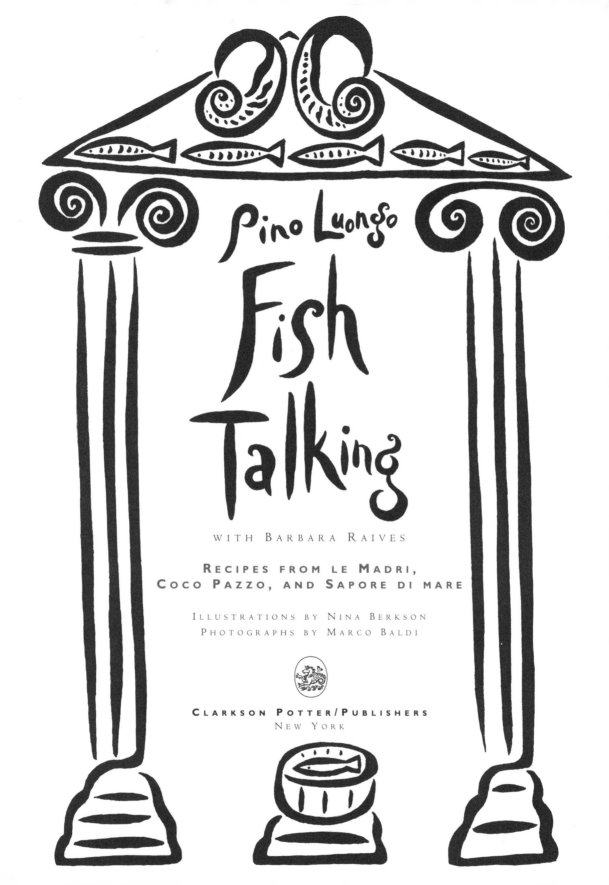

Pino Luongo

Fish Talking

WITH BARBARA RAIVES

RECIPES FROM LE MADRI,
COCO PAZZO, AND SAPORE DI MARE

ILLUSTRATIONS BY NINA BERKSON
PHOTOGRAPHS BY MARCO BALDI

CLARKSON POTTER/PUBLISHERS
NEW YORK

Thanks to Marta Pulini, Massimo Fiorillo, Mark Strausman, and Roy Finamore, for helping to make this book possible.
—Pino Luongo

Copyright © 1994 by Giuseppe Luongo
Illustrations copyright © 1994 by Nina Berkson

Published by Clarkson N. Potter, Inc.
201 E. 50th Street, New York, New York 10022. Member of the Crown Publishing Group.

Random House, Inc., New York, Toronto, London, Sydney, Auckland

CLARKSON N. POTTER, POTTER, and colophon are trademarks of Clarkson N. Potter, Inc.

Manufactured in the United States of America

DESIGN BY NANCY STEINY

Library of Congress Cataloging-in-Publication Data
Luongo, Pino.
Fish talking: recipes from le Madri, Coco Pazzo, and Sapore di mare/by
Pino Luongo with Barbara Raives; illustrations by Nina Berkson; photographs by
Marco Baldi.
p. cm.
1. Cookery (Fish) 2. Cookery, Italian. 3. le Madri (Restaurant) 4. Coco Pazzo
(Restaurant) 5. Sapore di mare (Restaurant)
I. Raives, Barbara. II Title.
TX747.L85 1994
641.6'92—dc20   93-31297
ISBN 0-517-59352-1   CIP

10 9 8 7 6 5 4 3 2 1

First Edition

CONTENTS

Fish Talking

INTRODUCTION

WITHOUT MY KNOWING IT THIS BOOK GOT STARTED IN THE WALK-IN COOLER OF MY FIRST RESTAURANT IN NEW YORK CITY. It was a hot summer night, and the restaurant was packed with customers. Maybe I was tired or too preoccupied with business, but I couldn't stand to look at all those mouths chewing, even though I was very pleased that everyone was enjoying the food. Whatever the reason, I decided I had to find a place where no one could reach me, and the only place that came to mind was the walk-in refrigerator in the basement.

I went downstairs hoping to grab a few minutes of peace and quiet. It was cool, and it smelled good. The lights were on, and the produce and meats were all in their places on the bottom shelves. But my attention was drawn to the fish on the upper shelves. They were in open cartons in tidy rows, like display boxes in a department store where all the ties and socks and shirts are neatly lined up for customers to admire. But here there were mackerel, red mullet, anchovies, and sardines that had arrived fresh from Italy that morning. All the eyes were looking at me, and I felt as if I were back in Italy surrounded by Italians. That's what I had been missing! I didn't have Italy and Italian people around me, so I settled for a walk-in box and Italian fish.

I discovered that the eyes of the red mullet have a pitifully mournful expression, unlike the anchovy, which looks bright and smart like a fox of the ocean. And the round little sea robins reminded me of a plump professor from my university days in Rome. They looked so alive that for a moment I felt I could talk to them.

What struck me most was that I had come from a room where many faces were chewing and laughing and talking, creating waves of life and energy. In contrast, these fish faces looked rested and relaxed, and even though I imagined they knew they were destined for the pan, they appeared to be approaching it in an untroubled way.

Don't we look relaxed?

For the last several months I have been getting together with the chefs from my three New York–area restaurants for fish talk. We have come up with menus and recipes that concentrate on the lesser-known, common folks of the sea that we are familiar with in Italy. In this book we pay most attention to these tasty, economical, and underrated fish and ignore (mostly) the classic tuna, swordfish, snapper, and bass that are promoted at the fish markets and restaurants in the United States.

There are two reasons that we offer these unassuming little guys, so well regarded in Tuscany, for consideration by our American friends: one, they are economical, and two, they offer a refreshing change of taste from their more imposing cousins.

Each one of my chefs has submitted recipes that focus on the "small" fish that they serve in their restaurants. Although Mark Strausman of Coco Pazzo is not a native Tuscan I made him an Italian by adoption. Coco Pazzo specializes in rich, gutsy fish stews and large portions of one-dish meals. We offer guests at Coco Pazzo the next best thing to eating in an Italian home.

Sapore di mare means "taste of the sea," and chef Massimo Fiorillo is well trained in the history of Italian cuisine. Massimo comes from a family that has been in the restaurant business in Liguria all his life, and he is familiar with all the dishes from his motherland, the great red pasta with shad roe and zucchini, the mackerel dishes he promised to make when I interviewed him for the job. When I said to him, "Let's use sardines, let's use anchovies, sea robins, mackerel, and everything else we use in Italy," he knew exactly what I was talking about.

The delicate touch of the slightly sophisticated Marta Pulini at le Madri creates fish dishes with a strong Italian accent that she presented like clothes in a fashion show.

Marta is from Modena, and she knows how to deal with all the fish from the Adriatic. The Adriatic offers eels, sardines, and all the little rough fish we use in Tuscany for stews and soups or serve just sautéed. Marta has a very modern, feminine approach to seafood, and many of her dishes are steamed or poached and served with herbs and vegetables.

I have taken each recipe in the book on its own merits and for its individual application. For example, I suggest that you serve Mark's *cacciucco* to six people because you can only have good results with a large variety of fish and shellfish, plenty of tomatoes to create a rich stock, and lots of toasted garlic bread to soak up the juices. It doesn't make sense to make it for one or two people. On the other hand, Marta's recipes for anchovies and sardines are worth making for one person. (How many can you eat? I suggest six because I love them. But it's up to you.)

I have included recipes that use fresh anchovies in season as well as anchovies preserved in salt, which you can buy in a big tin and keep in the refrigerator practically forever. Rinse as many as you want, put them in olive oil and garlic, add a sprinkle of parsley, and you will have the best snack in the world. They are always there for you to make a last-minute *bruschetta* with anchovies or a last-minute *spaghetti alla puttanesca*.

I suggest to cooks, professional and amateur, that you take full advantage of ingredients used in these recipes when they are in season. Stuff yourself with them every day for the two weeks or month that they are available fresh and consider them precious moments of your gastronomical life. In my book *A Tuscan in the Kitchen* I didn't tell you to eat porcini when they weren't in season, and I am not going to tell you here to eat a fish that is not in season, because it's probably frozen.

Shellfish are the exception. They are the jewels of the sea and taste great every season of the year, so I do plenty of work around mussels, clams, shrimp, and squid tossed with pasta and in fish and shellfish stews. But I don't only think of them as toss and combine. I let them stand on their own. There is nothing wrong with serving a major-size bowl of clams or mussels steamed in their own juices with a little garlic as a main course. That's the way we eat them in Italy in the summertime.

C O O K I N G   F I S H

When you buy fish, ask the fishmonger to scale, split, and clean the fish but to leave the head on. When you are preparing the noble tuna or swordfish, you are dealing with an anonymous chunk of body, but these more humble little guys of the sea need to keep their heads. Maybe they know they look better in a well-cooked dish, on a beautiful plate. Their color is better with fresh tomatoes; they look beautiful with vegetables. They need their heads so they can enjoy their surroundings.

It's my belief that no exact timing can be given as far as cooking fish, so whether you're roasting, poaching, broiling, grilling, or stewing fish, throw away your clock and depend on the two most important timers in your kitchen: the fork and your eyes. You'll need the fork to gently pierce the fish, to feel when it is firm but not tough, still tender but resists slightly when it is pierced. And you'll need your eyes to see if the flesh is white and smooth, a bright, milky color.

Fish cooks quickly, especially the small fish in this book. You should start watching to see if it is turning white after about three, four, or five minutes and then start touching it with your fork. I'm not asking you to stand next to the pot for hours, prodding the fish until it cries for mercy. In fact, you and the fish will be a lot happier if you don't. You don't want to injure the fish so it will fall apart before even making its way into your mouth. You want it to be firm and white. That's when it wants to be eaten.

When broiling, roasting, or grilling fish, start watching and poking when the skin begins to turn dark and gets crisp; or if it is filleted, when the outside begins to whiten. If you are boiling the fish or cooking it in a sauce, stir it around gently after two or three minutes to see if it is holding firm as it swims in the liquid. Look into the pot, inhaling the fragrance if you are cooking it in a sauce as you watch for it to turn white.

You don't need a clock if you depend on your senses and keep a fork handy and your eyes open. With the help of these essential tools the fish will tell you when it's ready.

STOCKING A TUSCAN KITCHEN

As in *A Tuscan in the Kitchen*, we give you here a list of the "must" items you should always have on hand in your pantry and refrigerator. With these essentials on hand, all you have to do is run out and grab the fresh items that give each dish its individual character. This idea of stocking the pantry applies to all other regional cooking of Italy.

PANTRY

Almonds
Anchovies
Beans—chickpeas, lentils, cannellini, black beans, red beans, lima beans
Bread crumbs
Capers
Cinnamon
Coriander—seeds and ground
Cornmeal, yellow
Flour—all-purpose and pastry
Herbs, dried (for when fresh are unavailable)
Juniper berries
Nutmeg
Oil—corn and olive
Olives—black and green, Gaeta or Nicoise
Pasta—penne, tubettini, farfalle, rotelle, rigatoni, spaghetti
Pepper—black, cayenne, crushed red
Pignolis
Porcini, dried
Raisins
Rice, Arborio (or long-grain Italian rice)

Salt
Sugar
Tomatoes—imported canned plum, tomato paste
Vinegar—red wine, white wine, balsamic
Walnuts
Wine—red, white, vermouth

COLD STORAGE

Broth—chicken, beef, fish, vegetable
Butter, unsalted
Carrots
Celery
Eggs
Garlic
Lemons
Milk
Onions, red
Parmesan cheese
Parsley (always fresh)
Potatoes
Shallots

To make life easier, I've divided the ingredients in the recipes by places they're kept in the Tuscan kitchen.

Items that can be stored without refrigeration because they are not perishable or because they are dried are **PANTRY** (*La Dispensa*) items. Look for the open tin and mason jar.

Ingredients that require refrigeration are called **COLD STORAGE** (*La Cantina*) items. Look for the open refrigerator.

At this point, if you have a pantry and refrigerator well stocked with those items you will use repeatedly, all you need to do to prepare is buy those few fresh items—most important the fresh fish—from the **MARKET** (*La Mercato*). Look for the shopping basket.

CHAPTER 1

For the Rich, for the Poor

SOME PEOPLE HAVE BIG PROJECTS, SOME PEOPLE HAVE BIG FORTUNES, AND SOME PEOPLE JUST HAVE A DREAM. I HAVE A DREAM THAT HAS BASICALLY GUIDED MY ACTIONS SINCE I CAME TO THIS COUNTRY, and which had its roots in the summer holidays I spent with my grandfather Bo. Nonno Bo was a fisherman, and his family owned many fishing boats, but he was also a Socialist, so he shared his wealth with the other fishermen.

Nonno Bo taught me many things on the summer days I spent with him at Laguna di Orbetello on the coast of southern Tuscany. When the fishing boats came back to the docks at the end of the day, the fish were unloaded and separated by size and type. As Nonno Bo sorted them out, he would always repeat the same thing over and over: "This one for them, the rich; this one for us, the poor; this for the rich; this for the poor."

Besides being a great fisherman, Bo was a great talker. Sometimes it was hard to tell if Bo was talking fish or philosophy. He would say, "Somehow the rich and the poor never have anything to say to each other; even when they are walking down the same street and come face-to-face, they don't talk. As close as they might be, it seems like they are hundreds of miles and thousands of years apart. But at least here, in our little town in our little village, one thing brings them all together: the fish.

"They all come to us for fish," Nonno Bo used to say, "and if you close your eyes and listen hard you can tell who they are by the fish they buy. If you hear, 'I want the striped bass,' you know it is the rich lady who comes to buy the most expensive fish, not only for the quality and type, but also for size. And with your eyes still closed, you can tell when the fisherman and the blue-collar wife and the peasant and the worker

Three lucky guys.

come, because they ask for sardines and anchovies and the hard crabs that make great soups. The rich are so predictable. All they do with the fish is grill it or poach it. They don't need fantasy, they don't need magic, they've got money." I stayed close to him hoping to capture whatever magic there was in his life.

P A N I N O   C O N   A C C I U G H E

M A R I N A T E D   A N C H O V Y   S A N D W I C H E S

8 *whole anchovies or*
16 *fillets, preserved*
  in salt or oil
Olive oil
Crushed red pepper

1 *garlic clove, sliced*
4 *parsley sprigs, chopped*
  coarsely
1 *garlic clove, peeled*

4 *slices country bread*

If you are using whole anchovies, fillet them: cut down the center, butterfly, and remove the spine bone. Trim the small bones from the sides of the fillets. Rinse them well in cold water, especially if you are using salt-preserved anchovies.

Lay the anchovies on a shallow platter and sprinkle them with the sliced garlic. Drizzle with olive oil until all the anchovies are covered. Sprinkle with the parsley and crushed red pepper to taste. Marinate in the refrigerator for 24 hours.

To make the sandwiches, toast or grill the bread. Rub the whole garlic clove around the crust of the toasted slices. Top each slice with 4 fillets and drizzle with olive oil.

M A K E S   4   S A N D W I C H E S

A N T I P A S T O   D I   A C C I U G H E ,   U O V A ,   E   C A P P E R I

M A R I N A T E D   A N C H O V I E S   W I T H   E G G S   A N D   C A P E R S

Serve this as an appetizer or light lunch with a good country bread.

8 whole anchovies or 16
  fillets, preserved in
  salt or oil
8 capers, finely chopped
4 tablespoons/60 ml olive oil
Salt
Pepper

½ medium onion,
  finely chopped
4 parsley sprigs,
  chopped coarsely
Juice of ½ lemon
4 eggs, hard-cooked

If you are using whole anchovies, fillet them: cut down the center, butterfly, and remove the spine bone. Trim the small bones from the sides of the fillets. Rinse them well in cold water, especially if you are using salt-preserved anchovies.

In a small bowl, toss together the anchovies, onion, parsley, and capers. In a separate bowl, mix the lemon juice, olive oil, salt, and pepper to make a dressing.

Peel the eggs and cut them in half. Arrange them on a serving platter. Cover with the anchovies and drizzle with the dressing.

S E R V E S   4

B O   D I E D   I N   1 9 7 0 when I was seventeen years old, but I can still picture those fish being taken out of the water, into the boat, out of the boat, into the boxes, and onto the shelves of the market, where they were split up and sold to the rich, to the poor. Although they all required the same amount of time and energy to be fished out of the water and put on the shelves, an arbitrary selection made some fish more important than others.

Pasta all in a row.

Although I didn't know it many years ago on the fishing docks of Orbetello, Bo was going to be involved in my future life.

When I came to New York in 1980, I decided I was going to be a restaurateur and a damned good one. Nonno Bo's distinction between the fish for the rich and the fish for the poor was the reason for my determination to bring to America the food of the peasant, which still feeds the Tuscan people. When I opened Il Cantinori, my first restaurant, I brought this concept to the dining tables of New York and offered dishes that would give my customers full appreciation of the food and culture of a civilization that they might know only through the dining table. I have succeeded in almost every flavor. I get New Yorkers to eat chicken livers; I get them to eat tripe; I encourage them to taste bread soups. I get them to eat all sorts of things that the undeveloped American palate never knew. I am as determined as ever to help Americans understand the pleasures of the humble anchovy, the fresh sardine, the red mullet, the shad, so that they will consider the small fish of importance equal to the tuna, the swordfish, and the snapper.

S A R D E   I M P A N A T E
B A K E D   S A R D I N E S

6 tablespoons / 72 g bread crumbs
1 tablespoon / 15 ml olive oil, plus more for garnish
Salt
Pepper

1 small garlic clove, finely chopped
3 parsley sprigs, chopped coarsely
Juice of ½ lemon
2 lemons, halved

12 fresh sardines, gutted, filleted, and butterflied, heads removed

Preheat the oven to 450°F/230°C.

In a mixing bowl, mix the bread crumbs and 1 tablespoon/15 ml olive oil. Add the garlic, parsley, lemon juice, and salt and pepper to taste. Mix well.

Oil a large baking sheet. Dip the sardines into the bread-crumb mixture, making sure they are well coated. Place them on the sheet and bake until golden brown, about 10 minutes. Transfer the sardines to a serving platter, drizzle with olive oil, garnish with lemon halves, and serve immediately.

S E R V E S   4

O R E C C H I E T T E   A L L A   S I C I L I A N A
P A S T A   W I T H   F R E S H   T U N A ,   S I C I L I A N - S T Y L E

½ *pound/250 g orecchiette*
¼ *cup/60 ml olive oil*
12 capers
12 black olives, pitted

6 plum tomatoes
*4 ounces/120 g fresh
   tuna*
3 oregano sprigs, chopped

In a large stockpot, boil salted water to cook the pasta. When the water is boiling, add the pasta. Dice the tomatoes and tuna. Add the olive oil to a large frying pan over medium heat. When the oil is hot, toss in the tomatoes, capers, olives, oregano, and tuna and cook for 2 minutes, being careful not to overcook the fish. Remove from the heat and set aside while you cook the pasta. Adjust the seasonings, if necessary. When the pasta is al dente, drain it and toss well with the sauce. Serve immediately.

S E R V E S   2

W H E N   I ' M   T A L K I N G   A B O U T   small fish, I'm not just talking about size; I'm talking about status. I'm talking about the modest fish, the unrespected, the fish that are not sufficiently appreciated.

Bo would be happy to know that in my restaurants many of my customers have finally acknowledged the background, the skill, and the imagination that goes into the simple fish recipes of the poor. There are restaurateurs who would like to have famous paintings on their walls. Others would like to know everybody and have everybody know them. I just want to serve fish with the heads on.

C E F A L O   A L L A   G R I G L I A   C O N   S A L S A   P I C C A N T E
G R I L L E D   B L U E F I S H   W I T H   S P I C Y   S A U C E

2 tablespoons / 30 ml olive oil
¼ teaspoon / 1 g crushed red
  pepper
2 cups / 500 ml canned
  crushed Italian plum tomatoes
Salt
Pepper
Vegetable oil

1 garlic clove, sliced
4 parsley sprigs, finely chopped

1 pound / 500 g bluefish,
  heads on, butterflied

In a saucepan over medium heat, cook the garlic in olive oil until golden brown. Add the crushed red pepper and tomatoes and simmer until the mixture has thickened slightly. Add the parsley and season to taste with salt and pepper. Set aside to cool.

Heat the grill to medium. Brush it lightly with vegetable oil. Lay the fish on the grill, opened up, skin side down, being careful not to put the fish on direct flame. Cook for 7 minutes. Do not turn. Arrange the fish on a platter, garnish with the sauce, and serve immediately.

S E R V E S   4

T HIS IS A GREAT BUSINESS if you do it with imagination and don't lose the desire to be creative. The theater taught me never to rest on the success of today; tomorrow you have to start all over again. And so eight restaurants later, here I am still thinking about Nonno Bo and trying to promote the unpretentious, unassuming, unwanted, nobody-cares-about-them little guys of the sea.

S G O M B R O   B O L L I T O   C O N   M A I O N E S E
P O A C H E D   M A C K E R E L   W I T H   M A Y O N N A I S E

It's not necessary to use extra virgin olive oil to make this mayonnaise.

F O R   T H E   F I S H

½ cup / 125 ml white wine
1 bay leaf
4 black peppercorns
Olive oil for serving

½ carrot, chopped coarsely
1 celery stalk, chopped coarsely
½ medium onion, chopped
  coarsely
4 parsley sprigs

4 small mackerel fillets
(10 to 12 inches / 25 to
30 cm each)

F O R   T H E   M A Y O N N A I S E

Dash of Worcestershire sauce
1 cup / 250 ml olive oil
Salt
Pepper

4 egg yolks
1 whole egg
Juice of 1 lemon

Poach the fish in a large shallow pan (or a fish poacher, if you have one). Place the wine, carrot, celery, onion, and 2 cups/500 ml water in the pan. Bring to a boil, then add the parsley, bay leaf, and peppercorns. Lay the mackerel fillets on top, lower the heat to medium, cover, and poach until tender. Remove the fillets from the pan and set them aside to cool.

For the mayonnaise, whisk the egg yolks and whole egg until fluffy. Add the lemon juice and Worcestershire sauce, mix, and then slowly drizzle in the olive oil, a little at a time, mixing until the mayonnaise has thickened. If the mayonnaise becomes too thick, add a tablespoon or two of cold water and whisk well. Season to taste with salt and pepper.

To serve, arrange the mackerel on a serving platter. Drizzle lightly with olive oil and garnish with parsley, if desired. Serve with the mayonnaise.

S E R V E S   4

*Morning delivery to
le Madri.*

CHAPTER 2

Puttanesca in Queens

W HEN I LANDED IN NEW YORK IN OCTOBER 1980 THE FIRST THING I ASKED MYSELF WAS, HOW SOON CAN I GET OUT OF HERE? THE SECOND WAS, WHAT AM I GOING TO EAT?

Three days into my new life in America, I moved into an apartment somewhere in Ozone Park, leased to me by a family of Yugoslavian immigrants. I arrived by subway, and it didn't take me long to register the differences between Queens and the beautiful squares and old streets of Rome.

The moment that the subway emerged from the tunnel on the Queens side of the East River I could see the rooftops of the square, brown houses on both sides of the train, one next to the other, lining the railroad tracks. I felt like I was in a scene from a King Kong movie where this big "boonga-boonga" gorilla is standing on the tracks between buildings that reach only as high as his chest. As the elevated train speeds by him, he grabs it in one gigantic fist and splits it in half as though it were a toy. Queens looked like a toy town to me.

The neighborhood was unlike anything I had ever seen living in Rome among Romans or Tuscany among Tuscans, who all speak with the same accents and gesticulate in familiar ways. The streets were filled with every sort of person. Every color, every language, every way of dressing that a human being can imagine was there in Ozone Park. And none of it looked familiar to me.

Before I went to bed that first night I turned on the TV to practice my English and found Ronald Reagan, soon to become president, on network TV. I knew him as an actor, and it took me a few minutes to make the connection: this guy was not acting; he was running for president. I went to sleep with the comforting thought that even an actor can run for president in the United States.

But the real struggle began the next day when I decided I wanted to eat. Picture me entering this gigantic supermarket, the guy who went to the little markets in Rome and bought everything fresh from street vendors with carts. Vegetables from one, fish from another, meat from a third, a stop at the baker on the way home. It seemed to me on entering that supermarket that every possible thing that could kill you was there, and all that poison was not even offered up with charm. Everything was on shelves; everything had its own number and price; everything was labeled with the name of the product; everything was wrapped in plastic—and it was all unrecognizable. It was a food nightmare.

In the supermarket, you go to the meat counter where you have no idea which cut comes from which part of the animal. You just see little strips of scallopini, chops, ribs, all wrapped up and sealed. There are no pictures of the whole animal like we have in Europe, and you won't get an explanation from those shadowy figures behind the glass partition. I guess many years of supermarket exposure have made Americans identify meat by its color; beef is red, pork is pink, and veal is white. Think about all the chicken and turkey and game that are covered with plastic and look as if they are wearing a tight dress. The label on the package says "I'm a duck" or "I'm a guinea hen," so you buy a label and try to imagine what's inside.

And the nightmare gets worse when you move to what is called the vegetable department. (It should really be called the condomized vegetable department because everything comes with plastic protection.) It is the most unappetizing, disrespectful, ignorant abuse of the oldest way of doing business that I know. Historically, the farmer has always worked the land and delivered the produce to the distributor; the distributor got it to the store, and the store sold it to the customer. The farmers were at the beginning of the chain, and at the other end were the consumers. The products in between were never altered; they were bought fresh and sold fresh.

In the supermarket, I felt like I was facing a time in the future when people do not eat real food anymore. Oh yes, the apples are perfect; I've never seen such shiny apples! Not even my shoes have ever been so shiny.

Let's fillet . . .

But there is none of the character of something that has been grown and cared for and sold for the purpose of giving health and pleasure to the consumer. To me it is just stuff grouped by size and wrapped in plastic. And variety—zero. Romaine and iceberg lettuce—but where is my arugula, where is my radicchio? Where is my fresh basil and *rughetta?* Those first two weeks in America were really depressing.

Rolling the pasta.

But somehow you have to survive, somehow you have to eat, so you buy something in plastic. You bring it home, store it in the refrigerator, and when you finally take the plastic off, you regret that you bought it in the first place. There is no life inside because the plastic stops everything from breathing. So now you have a tasteless, smell-less thing that at one time grew in the ground and was meant to be eaten, but it has traveled so far, and so many hands have handled it on the way to the customer, that now it is just a sad interpretation of a vegetable. How was I going to make my beautiful vegetable soup, my pasta, my fish, my meat dishes without any real vegetables?

After facing the vegetable department and the meat department, out of respect to Nonno Bo's memory I refused to even peek at the fish department.

I wanted to keep my first meal simple, so I decided to make pasta. That should have been easy enough. I looked at all the brands at the supermarket, and all I could see was Ronzoni and Mueller, Mueller and Ronzoni. I could live with Ronzoni, it sounded Italian, but when I saw the name Mueller I thought, That's not going to work; a German making pasta? So after a long, philosophical moment, I chose to go with the Italian. Sometimes it is important to trust your instincts.

Now I needed the ingredients for sauce. I looked for capers, canned anchovies, herbs, and spices. The spice shelf looked just like the cigarette shelf, with little boxes of the same size, all neatly lined up. Everything was dry, and everything was sealed. I paid the bill and moved toward my first home-cooked meal in America.

That evening I managed to make a decent *puttanesca* sauce. A guy from Rome living in Ozone Park on a sublease from a Yugoslavian immigrant family, cooking Ronzoni spaghetti.

SPAGHETTI ALLA PUTTANESCA
WHORE-STYLE SPAGHETTI

3 whole anchovies or 6 fillets,
  preserved in salt or oil
1 pound/500 g spaghetti
3 tablespoons/45 ml olive oil
2 cups/500 ml canned whole
  Italian tomatoes
6 capers
6 black olives, pitted
Crushed red pepper
Salt
Pepper

1 garlic clove, sliced

If you are using whole anchovies, fillet them: cut down the center, butterfly, and remove the spine bone. Trim the small bones from the sides of the fillets. Rinse them in cold water, especially if you are using salt-preserved anchovies. Cut each into quarters.

In a large stockpot, bring salted water to a boil for the pasta.

In a frying pan over medium heat, cook the garlic in the olive oil until golden brown. Add the anchovies and cook for a moment. Add the tomatoes and simmer slowly.

Add the pasta to the boiling water. While the pasta is cooking, add the capers, olives, and crushed red pepper to taste to the sauce. Season with salt and pepper and continue simmering. If the sauce gets too thick, add a spoonful of the pasta water.

When the pasta is al dente, drain and toss it well with the sauce. Serve immediately.

SERVES 4

S P A G H E T T I   M A L A F E M M I N A

S P A G H E T T I   B A D   G I R L – S T Y L E

4 whole anchovies or 8 fillets,
  preserved in salt or oil

1 pound / 500 g spaghetti

3 tablespoons / 45 ml olive oil

8 capers

Crushed red pepper

Salt

Pepper

1 garlic clove, sliced

4 plum tomatoes, diced

4 ounces / 120 g fresh
  mozzarella, cut into
  cubes

If you are using whole anchovies, fillet them: cut down the center, butterfly, and remove the spine bone. Trim the small bones from the sides of the fillets. Rinse them well in cold water, especially if you are using salt-preserved anchovies. Cut them into quarters.

In a large stockpot, bring salted water to a boil for the pasta.

In a frying pan over medium heat, cook the garlic in the olive oil until golden brown. Add the anchovies and cook for a moment. Add the tomatoes and simmer until the sauce has thickened slightly. Add the capers and crushed red pepper, salt, and pepper to taste. Cook for a few minutes more. If the sauce gets too thick, add a spoonful of the pasta water.

Cook the pasta in the boiling water until al dente. Drain and toss well with the sauce. Top with the mozzarella and serve immediately.

S E R V E S   4

SPAGHETTI CON ACCIUGHE IN BIANCO
SPAGHETTI WITH ANCHOVIES AND GARLIC

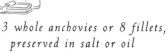

3 whole anchovies or 8 fillets,
  preserved in salt or oil
1 pound / 500 g spaghetti
3 tablespoons / 45 ml olive oil
Salt
Pepper

2 garlic cloves, sliced
4 parsley sprigs, chopped
  coarsely

If you are using whole anchovies, fillet them: cut down the center, butterfly, and remove the spine bone. Trim the small bones from the sides of the fillets. Rinse them in cold water, especially if you are using salt-preserved anchovies. Cut each into quarters.

In a large stockpot, boil salted water. When the water is boiling, add the pasta. While it is cooking, quickly make the sauce.

In a frying pan, cook the garlic in the olive oil until golden brown. Add the anchovies and cook until they start to melt. Remove the pan from the heat.

When the pasta is al dente, drain it, reserving a small amount of the pasta water. Add the pasta to the anchovies. Toss for a moment over medium heat, season with salt and pepper to taste. If the anchovy mixture is too thick, add a spoonful of pasta water. Toss until all the spaghetti is coated. Garnish with parsley and serve immediately.

SERVES 4

I HAVE COME A LONG WAY since that night in Queens. I had no choice.

When I put that meal together that night, the concoction of ingredients and the situation were so incongruous that there were only two ways left for me to go. I could open the window and jump, or I could close the window and go to sleep and look for work the next morning. I chose the second.

The few acquaintances and friends I had in Manhattan suggested that I just go around and ask for a job. I started on the Upper East Side on Sixty-first Street, where a friend of a friend told me he knew some Italian people who owned a small clothing store. At last, someone who could speak my language. I had been buried in a week of silence. After a very short interview—which consisted mainly of "Where do you come from? I'm from the north, you're from the south, we never met in Italy, let's meet now, let's go ahead with our lives, give me a job because I'm starving to death"—I got the job.

Basically the work consisted of vacuuming the carpet and cleaning the windows in the morning and then . . . waiting. Wait for lunch, and after lunch . . . wait again. Then came closing hour, and things had to be put away and dusted. Close the store, get on the subway, and wait again to get to Ozone Park, where I would make a quick sandwich before falling into bed.

P A N I N O   C O N   T O N N O
T U N A   S A N D W I C H

One 6-ounce / 180-g can
   Italian tuna, packed in oil
4 tablespoons / 20 ml olive oil
Salt
Pepper

1 small red onion,
   thinly sliced

4 pieces focaccia (each
   about 2 by 2 inches)
1 large beefsteak tomato,
   sliced

Drain the tuna. Place the tuna in a small bowl and add 2 tablespoons/30 ml of the olive oil and salt and pepper to taste. Mix well.

Slice the focaccia in half lengthwise. Drizzle the slices with the remaining olive oil, spread with the tuna, and top with tomato and onion slices. Close the sandwiches and serve.

SERVES 4

PANE FRITTO CON ALICI
FRIED BREAD WITH ANCHOVIES

I suggest smaller pieces if you're using this as an hors d'oeuvre, larger ones if you're serving it with a meal.

*Anchovies, preserved in salt,
  filleted*
Olive oil

*Bread dough, homemade or
  frozen, raw*

Rinse the anchovies and cut into pieces ½ inch to 1 inch long.

Roll out the bread dough to ¼-inch thickness. Place anchovy pieces on top of half of the dough and cover by folding over the other half. Using a pizza cutter, cut the dough into small pieces in whatever shape you prefer (rectangle, triangle, baguette, et cetera). Set aside, covered with a cloth, for half an hour.

Heat ½ inch of oil in a heavy frying pan until very hot. Fry the dough, turning once, until brown. Drain briefly on paper towels and serve very hot.

P A N I N O   C O N   F O N T I N A   E   A C C I U G H E

A N C H O V Y   A N D   F O N T I N A   S A N D W I C H

8 whole anchovies or 16 fillets, preserved in salt or oil
6 tablespoons / 90 ml olive oil

8 slices Italian Fontina or Bel Paese
4 parsley sprigs, chopped

4 pieces focaccia (each about 2 by 2 inches)

If you are using whole anchovies, fillet them: cut down the center, butterfly, and remove the spine bone. Trim the small bones from the sides of the fillets. Rinse them well in cold water, especially if you are using salt-preserved anchovies.

Lay the anchovies on a plate, drizzle them with 4 tablespoons / 60 ml of the olive oil, and marinate them at room temperature for 2 hours.

Preheat the oven to 400°F/200°C. To make the sandwiches, slice the focaccia in half lengthwise. Brush with the remaining olive oil. On each piece lay 2 anchovy fillets and top with a slice of cheese. Place them on a baking sheet and bake until the cheese is melted. Sprinkle with the chopped parsley and serve hot.

S E R V E S   4

F O R *I L   P A N I N O   D E L   M A R I N A I O,* or The Sailor's Sandwich, I would cut country bread into thin slices. For each sandwich, I would layer tomato, onion—sliced very thin—several leaves of basil, then anchovy fillets on a slice of bread. On another slice of bread, I'd spread a tablespoon of olive oil, a pinch of salt, and a bit of dried oregano. I would close the sandwich, press it, cut it in half, and devour it.

I lasted in the job for two and a half days. The first day I told myself I had to be positive. At the end of the second day I told myself I just had to be positive for another week. The third day I got on the subway, thinking about how to be positive, walked into the store, saw the vacuum cleaner and the windows waiting for me, and said, "Screw positive." I left. I didn't even have the guts to ask for my two days salary; I just walked away, heading south.

I told myself that there had to be some logic to Manhattan. High-rise buildings meant walls and distances between people who didn't have time to talk to me and think about what this Italian wanted. But it couldn't all be like that. So slowly my feet took me downtown, and when I saw the architecture change from high-rises to brownstones, then from brownstones to little shops, I said to myself, Ah! This is of a human dimension, I can relate to this, I like this part of town, it feels good to be here.

So nice. So neat.

When I reached Greenwich Village, I stopped at a little restaurant on Sixth Avenue and looked in the window at the menu. A bell rang in my head. Here were words that came from Tuscany: *crostini di caccia, crostini di fegato, ribollita, pappa al pomodoro, panzanella.* I said to myself, I have found someone who knows where he comes from. I went inside and asked if there was a job—any job—available. When the manager asked if I had ever worked in a restaurant, I said never, but that I had eaten in restaurants all my life. I knew Italian food very well, and I knew how to deal with people. I got the job.

I was pleased to be in the Village, and I looked forward to getting up in the morning and going to work. Working at the restaurant was hard work, but it gave me the sense of, as Nonno Bo would say, integrity, the dignity of the worker.

I guess the restaurant business was in my bones, because after two months of busing tables I was given the position that would change my life forever. I was offered the job of manager. My English was of the lowest level, but luckily I was moving so fast that I couldn't stay anywhere for a conversation that lasted for more than five words. My responses to whatever people said was a jovial "Ha-ha-ha, yes, sure, enjoy your dinner," but I didn't know if someone was being nice or not.

I worked there long enough to pay my dues—day and night, hour after hour, six days a week. I was beginning to learn the restaurant business—and the language.

CHAPTER 3

The Debut of the Small Guys

I THINK THE DAY THAT I FELT REALLY SET-
TLED INTO NEW YORK WAS THE DAY THAT I
WAS APPROACHED BY A FRIEND WHO SUGGESTED
THAT WE OPEN A RESTAURANT TOGETHER.
WHEN HE ASKED IF I COULD handle it, I said, "I know
how to cook, I know how to plan a menu, and I know how to deal with
people. I have trained busers and waiters; I can be a bartender or a
cashier. And if I have to, I can be a dishwasher."

The only thing I didn't know was that I would have to build the
restaurant from scratch. By the time I learned that "GC" meant "general
contractor," I was already in the construction business. Against all my
intentions I ended up designing and building Il Cantinori, my first, partially owned, but fully sweated, restaurant.

Il Cantinori was built with the idea of recapturing a piece of the
Italian countryside that I very much missed. After months of hard work,
a storehouse of personal dreams, and the desire for a better life in
America, we were ready to open. We opened without fanfare and music,
in a very modest way—like the modest fish of Nonno Bo—but the plus
was that I was in charge of everything. There wasn't an angle of the business that escaped my control. The menu was created by me, specials were
planned by me, waiters were trained by me, and customers were dealing
with me. It was a full-time, seven-days-a-week job, and I enjoyed it from
beginning to end.

Two or three months later, after the restaurant had been reviewed and
was successful, I started to play around with the little-known fish dishes
that I wanted to introduce to New Yorkers. On large tables near the
entrance I displayed beautiful platters of vegetables and tiny fish like
whitebait and whiting. I invited people to have a taste without charging
them, just to encourage them to try the more unusual dishes.

More for le Madri.

B I A N C H E T T I   I N   A G R O

P I C K L E D   W H I T E B A I T

Flour
Salt
Pepper
Vegetable oil
3½ cups/875 ml white wine
  vinegar (7 percent acidity)
6 black peppercorns
1 bay leaf
6 tablespoons/72 g sugar
Crushed red pepper

1 pound/500 g whitebait

In a shallow bowl, mix some flour with a little salt and pepper.

Heat the vegetable oil in a large, deep frying pan (or deep-fat fryer) over medium-high heat. Once the oil is hot (do not let the oil get so hot that it smokes), quickly dredge the whitebait in the flour mixture, a handful at a time. Fry until golden brown and remove to drain on paper towels. Repeat this process until all the whitebait are fried.

In a saucepan, add the vinegar, ½ cup/125 ml water, peppercorns, bay leaf, sugar, and some crushed red pepper to taste and bring to a rapid boil for several minutes. Cool.

In a separate saucepan, boil water to cover a 1-quart/1-l canning jar. Immerse the jar in the water for several minutes. Remove it from the water and dry it with a clean towel. While the jar is still hot, add the whitebait and then pour in the vinegar mixture to ½ inch/1 cm from the top of the jar. Top with a lid and ring.

Set the jar in a saucepan of cool water covering ¾ of the jar. (You may want to put a jar rack or an old tea towel in the bottom of the saucepan to keep the jar from jumping around as the water boils.) Bring the water to a boil and process for 15 minutes. Remove the jar and set it in a cool place. You will be able to tell when the jar is sealed, as it makes a "ping" sound. Store in a cool place to marinate for 3 months.

M A K E S   1   Q U A R T

IT WAS IMPORTANT for me to have these plebeians of the sea on hand at any given time because they kept me focused. Everyone has a favorite memory to fall back on when they are undergoing drastic changes. Some people remember their first day at school, other people remember their first love; for me it was my grandfather Nonno Bo. And nothing represented Nonno Bo better than the beloved, humble, little-known (in America) guys that he fished out of the sea. So there I was, the gracious host of Il Cantinori, fulfilling an obligation to Nonno Bo and featuring sardines, anchovies, and whitebait the way they really are when they get out of the water, not all canned and mashed so you can't even recognize them. I had a mission: to get my customers to appreciate these natural little ocean inhabitants that fed us so well in Italy.

The al dente station.

My conversion attempts caused a serious problem only once. One day I was really pushing with a very good customer of mine, and I told him that I loved anchovies so much I could eat them raw. When he challenged me, I felt like my whole personal history was at stake. I had to prove to him that I meant what I said. The fact is that I had never eaten fish raw, but I remembered how Nonno Bo used to do it. He would place his thumb and forefinger within the gills of the anchovy, put the fish in his mouth, and pull it through between his teeth. Pride got the better of me. I put the anchovy in my mouth and pulled it through. It was rough to keep a straight face, because even though the fish was fresh and the taste of the sea was there, I wasn't.

But it definitely had the desired effect on the customer. He no longer had trouble with the tiny bones in the anchovy, he had no problems with the heads of the whitebait; he devoured sardines flopped open and grilled with bread crumbs—as long as they were cooked he ate them all. I made a man out of this guy, that's what I did. I turned him into a person with a palate and a new vision of what food is all about. He was no longer just interested in swordfish steak and fillet of sole, fillet of snapper, and fillet of tuna; he had become acquainted with the sweet taste of Nonno Bo's modest little jewels of the sea. He should be indebted to me for the rest of his life.

A L I C I   C R U D E   M A R I N A T E   C O N   L I M O N E   E   O L I O

F R E S H   A N C H O V I E S   M A R I N A T E D   W I T H   L E M O N   A N D   O L I V E   O I L

Serve these with a good peasant bread.

Olive oil
Salt
Pepper

Juice of 1 lemon
6 parsley sprigs, coarsely
    chopped
2 garlic cloves, sliced

16 fresh anchovies,
    cleaned and butterflied

Lay the anchovies on a platter. Sprinkle them with lemon juice, olive oil, parsley, garlic, and salt and pepper to taste. Marinate the mixture in the refrigerator for 24 hours.

SERVES 4

ANY TRICK YOU CAN pull to get people to eat good food is worth it. The mental barrier that acts as a locked gate to their mouths is based on past experience. It is this false connection with old food prejudices that keeps people from enjoying food.

Conceiving, putting together, and writing my first menu was for me the equivalent of Dante writing the first chapter of *The Divine Comedy*. Like everything else in life there is so much you want to put into it that at one point you have to know how to say yes to this and no to that; yes for this dish and no to that one. I had a volcano in my mind spitting out recipes and dishes constantly. All I had to do was get the stove under control and make it generate so many appetizers, so many pastas, so many main courses. It was a very difficult undertaking. I think it took me longer to put together the first menu than it did to put together the staff of the whole restaurant, including dishwashers, cooks, busboys, and bartender. But when the restaurant was accepted with joy because everything on it was original and authentically Tuscan, I realized that the struggle was worth it.

I'm proud to say that Il Cantinori set a new standard for the Italian-restaurant scene in New York. It heralded a new generation of restaurateurs: no more wise guys with twisted noses, no more misspelled words on the menu, no more dishes that I had never heard of in Italy. Everything was just pure Tuscan cuisine.

But as happy as I was with Il Cantinori, my dilemma was still how to make the small, unwanted, modest, unpretentious, so-unlikely-to-become-popular fish a regular part of the menu. I always put them on the menu, and then I would see them sitting in the refrigerator for a day or two before being thrown away or incorporated into a risotto or pasta dish. Everything else was moving. The scallopini was moving. The pasta with this and that was moving. Even the chicken liver was moving. But the anchovies had to find a second life in the *puttanesca* sauce.

I remember day after day going through the early morning meeting with the chef. We talked about how we were going to butterfly these beautiful sardines, dust them with bread crumbs, flavor them with a little olive oil, lemon, and garlic, and put them under the broiler until they came up crunchy and sweet. Or how we were going to do these anchovies, just slightly open with the heads on, poached in a very light white wine sauce. My intention was to serve these fish two or three times a week, to offer customers a sense of what we really eat in Tuscany.

They are the honey of the sea, these little guys. I persevere because I have given up so many ways since I left my country that these things, which are so important to me, are really my way of hanging on to the Tuscany of my childhood.

Many of my customers travel to Tuscany, and they eat fish there they wouldn't eat here. Most of the restaurants serve the common, unsophisticated, inexpensive fish because the fancy snapper and tuna aren't around; the small guys are in charge over there. Travelers either accept the local dishes or they starve. So now my battle was developing on three fronts: One was in the dining room, where I was trying to push my fish from Tuscany, a little portion here, a little portion there. The second was abroad: if I can't win in my own dining room, and I find out you're going to Italy, I'll get you there. And the third was my battle with my own employees—my purchasing managers, my waiters, my chefs, who complained, "We prepare it, but we don't sell it." I was constantly telling them they had to prepare it, they had to put it on the menu, because you can't escape the plebeian little guys. They've got to be eaten; they deserve respect.

One of the best ways to endorse this respect is to introduce them to rice, to encourage them to form an alliance that will create great risotto, such as *Risotto con le Sarde e Finocchi* and *Risotto con Alici e Zafferano.* As you see, they are very elastic in the way they can be used.

Oops!

R I S O T T O   C O N   L E
S A R D E   E   F I N N O C H I

R I S O T T O   W I T H   F R E S H   S A R D I N E S
A N D   F E N N E L

¼ cup / 48 g bread crumbs
2 tablespoons / 30 ml olive oil
1 cup / 190 g Arborio rice
Salt
Pepper
1 cup / 250 ml white wine
1 cup / 250 ml fish (see page
  121) or vegetable stock

1 very small garlic clove, finely
  minced
Juice of 1 lemon
1 small onion, finely minced
2 tablespoons / 32 g butter

1 large or 2 small fennel
  bulbs, julienned
16 fresh sardines, cleaned,
  filleted, heads off, cut
  into quarters
4 dill sprigs, finely
  chopped

Heat the oven to 475°F/240°C.

In a small mixing bowl, toss together the bread crumbs, garlic, lemon juice, and olive oil until well mixed. Spread onto a baking sheet and place in the oven to brown for several minutes. Be sure not to overbrown, or they will taste burned. Remove the bread crumbs from the oven and set them aside.

In a large saucepan over medium heat, sauté the onion in the butter until wilted. Add the rice and salt and pepper to taste and stir until the rice is coated. Add half of the wine and stock. Cover and cook, checking occasionally to make sure the liquid has not completely evaporated. Keep adding more stock and wine as needed. After adding most of the stock and wine, add the fennel, stir, and cover again. Two or 3 minutes from the end, add the sardines and dill, mix gently, and cook until the fish is done and the rice is al dente. Turn out onto a serving platter, sprinkle with bread crumbs, and serve hot.

S E R V E S   4

RISOTTO CON ALICI
E ZAFFERANO

RISOTTO WITH ANCHOVIES AND SAFFRON

6 tablespoons/90 ml olive oil
1 tablespoon/12 g dried wild
  fennel or dill
Hot red pepper, dried or fresh
1½ cups/285 g Arborio rice
¼ cup/60 ml white wine
Pinch of saffron threads
Salt

1 garlic clove, minced
1 onion, thinly sliced
6 cups/1,5 l fish broth
  (see page 91)
1 tablespoon/12 g finely
  chopped parsley
2 tablespoons/24 g grated
  Pecorino

1 pound/500 g fresh
  anchovies
3 medium fresh tomatoes
½ cup/100 g fava beans,
  peeled and blanched

Skin, clean, and fillet the anchovies, removing the heads. Blanch the tomatoes in boiling water to loosen the skins. Peel, seed, and chop.

In a small saucepan, sauté the tomatoes in 4 tablespoons/60 ml of the olive oil. Add the anchovies, half the fava beans, half the fennel or dill, and hot red pepper to taste. Cook over medium heat until the fava beans are tender and the anchovies are cooked through. Set aside.

In a heavy saucepan over medium heat, sauté the garlic and onion until golden in 2 table-spoons/30 ml of olive oil. Add the rice, stirring until all the rice has been coated with oil. Add the white wine and cook until the wine evaporates. Add a ladle of fish broth and the saffron, stirring constantly. The mixture should be gently bubbling, but not boiling. Keep adding the broth a ladle at a time as the liquid evaporates. When the rice is tender to the bite, but not mushy, remove from the heat, add the uncooked fava beans, the remaining fennel or dill, parsley, and Pecorino cheese, and mix well. Taste for salt. Turn the risotto out onto a serving plate and spoon the anchovy-and-fava-bean mixture on top. Serve immediately.

SERVES 6

CHAPTER 4

Sand, Sun, Salt & Sea

ℬEFORE I OPENED SAPORE DI MARE I USED TO ENJOY SPENDING LONG WEEKENDS IN THE HAMPTONS. I NEEDED A PLACE TO GO NEAR THE WATER; I NEEDED TO SEE BEACHES, A LANDSCAPE THAT REMINDED ME of where I grew up. Even though the Hamptons don't bear any resemblance to the Mediterranean, just to see the wild, open beaches, feel the salt air, and swim in the ocean was inspiring.

My biggest pleasure was seeing the fishing boats come into Montauk loaded with big tuna, flukes, flounder, scrod, and mackerel. And my greatest joy was to see them represented in so many local restaurants.

After two years, I saw the future in a beautiful property for sale on Georgica Pond. The inside of the place looked like some kind of pestilence had come through, and all the inhabitants had dropped dead and disappeared in the middle of whatever they were doing. It was a shambles—dark, dirty, with traces of food everywhere. Although it was hard to conceive of doing it over, my desire to be there and seek justice for these little guys of the sea, who were now just a few miles away, allowed me to stretch my imagination and take a chance. I set to work turning this tomb into a beautiful temple of fish.

Sapore di mare took form early in 1988, and all the while we were cleaning up the restaurant and basically bringing back to life a once-beautiful building, I was thinking about what I was going to call it. A name for a restaurant is very important. It sets the theme. I wanted it to mean something to me first and then to the people who would come there.

Sapore di mare means "taste of the sea." It is a phrase from a great song of the sixties by Gino Paoli. Remember when you were a kid and school was out and you took a three- or four-month vacation? You were in the sea every day, and no matter how many showers you took the salt built up on your skin. I used to love sucking my arm just to get this flavor of salt and sea. That's what this song—and my restaurant—are about: sand, sun, salt, sea.

I had three older sisters and two younger brothers, and we spent every summer at the beach near Nonno Bo's house. In my patriarchal family there was no way that my sisters were going to have a summer nightlife without me going along. As I was the oldest son in the family, I was instructed by my father to accompany them everywhere. So beginning at the young age of thirteen I was having a ball. My sisters and I made a pact. We would leave the house together, go about five hundred yards, and—split. We would meet again in the same spot at the designated hour, compare notes, and agree on stories before going home together. This went on every summer for years.

What has this to do with small fish? It was summer, and summer always means fish to me. My mother would prepare fish at least three times a week. If it was a rainy day, we would hunt for snails in the pine woods and have a snail stew. Or if it wasn't snails, Nonno Bo would bring over eels, which would crop up in a soup. Fish were in the pasta sauce, served as a main course or in an appetizer, pickled, fried, smoked, stewed, grilled—some way that always made sense.

The art of garganelli.

S G O M B R O   C O N   P I S E L L I

M A C K E R E L   W I T H   P E A S

Olive oil
1 cup / 250 ml white wine
Salt

1 white onion, sliced
4 tablespoons / 65 g butter

½ pound / 250 g shelled
fresh peas (if fresh are
not available, substitute
frozen)
4 Boston mackerel, cleaned
and filleted

In a large sauté pan over medium heat, add just enough oil to coat the bottom of the pan. Add the onion and sauté until soft. Add the peas, cook for a few seconds, then add the white wine. Raise the heat and simmer until the wine has partially evaporated. Add enough water to cover the peas, reduce the heat, cover, and simmer gently for about 20 minutes, checking occasionally to see that the mixture is not drying out. Remove the lid and gently lay the mackerel on top of the peas. Add just enough water to keep the peas moist, cover, and cook over low heat for 8 to 10 minutes. Using a fork, test the fish for doneness (the fish should flake when touched with a fork). Sprinkle lightly with salt and place 1 tablespoon / 16 g butter on top of each fillet. Turn out onto plates, drizzle with olive oil, and serve immediately.

S E R V E S   4

D U R I N G   T H E   W I N T E R   M O N T H S of construction I knew exactly how I wanted Sapore di mare to be and how I would do it. We were building a stage to represent the best years of my life: being young, having three older sisters, having all the freedom and all the action that a young boy would want.

Sapore brings back all the great things about summer. The restaurant was built with a specific season in mind, a specific set of emotions and feelings and one desire: to convey what it means to have fun in the summer and what kind of food we like to eat in Tuscany. And so the temple of the plebeian fish was built and opened on May 23, 1988.

Pasta for six.

The menu featured pasta with sardines, pasta with anchovies, risotto with octopus, marinated eels, mussels, and clams. Long wooden tables displayed all of my favorite fish dishes: a nice plate of anchovies that had been gently butterflied, marinated in lemon juice, then covered with olive oil, garlic, and parsley and served at room temperature; a beautiful octopus salad, the tentacles boiled, sliced, and marinated in olive oil and lemon juice, sprinkled with parsley and a little zest of orange; a salad of fresh fava beans and mussels; whitebait, deep-fried and slightly pickled from being poached in white wine vinegar, garlic, and hot pepper, which you eat heads and all—we call them hundreds-in-the-mouth, that's how tiny they are.

F R I T T E L L E   D I   B I A N C H E T T I
S M A L L   W H I T E B A I T   C A K E S

2 cups / 280 g flour
White wine
Vegetable oil
Salt

¹/₂ cup / 100 g minced parsley
1 lemon, cut into wedges

1 pound / 500 g white-
  bait, cleaned and rinsed

In a mixing bowl, mix the flour with enough wine to make a *pastella* (slurry) with the consistency of thick cream. Add the parsley and mix well.

Heat about ¹/₂ inch/1 cm of oil in a frying pan over high heat. While the oil is heating, mix the whitebait quickly and gently with the flour mixture. Using a tablespoon, place spoonfuls of whitebait into the hot oil. There should be enough oil to cover the cakes; if not, add more oil, and wait until it is hot to add more batter to the pan. When the cakes are golden brown, remove them from the pan and place them on paper towels to drain off the excess oil. Sprinkle lightly with salt to taste, garnish with lemon wedges, and serve immediately.

S E R V E S   4

T HE CURTAIN WENT ON Sapore di mare with almost everything I wanted in place. It was a Mediterranean-style restaurant, white stucco, terra-cotta floors, different levels in the dining room, an open terrace next to the porch facing the pond, and another little terrace on the garden side. There was not one meat dish on the early menu. It was probably the most exciting menu I have ever put together.

A few weeks into the summer all my faithful customers came, the ones who had been following me since early days, and there were many of them. They were from every sort of business: the record business, the finance business, bankers, entrepreneurs, sleazebags, and some of uncertain, undefined businesses.

Couples of every age and combination were there. Women and men, young women with older men, young men with older women, male with female, male with male, female with female. They all combined in the big melting pot that was the Sapore di mare scene.

It was exciting for me to look at this rainbow of people of different backgrounds, needs, loves, passions, and tastes. To think that somehow I was capable of combining them in one large dining room, where they were willing to accept the food that I offered instead of the food they thought they wanted or expected in a restaurant owned by an Italian. Before my opera of persuasion there was a lot of silly Italian food around town, food that I call silly because even though it sounded Italian it never really connected to what Italian regional cuisine is all about.

When Sapore di mare opened, it was received in a very positive way from such a diverse representation of customers that it confirmed my theory that food is the great social leveler. The people who come to my restaurant have more in common than just eating. You can do that at any diner or McDonald's. But when you approach certain restaurants, you know you are going to have a dining experience: a combination of ambience and people socializing and enjoying food. It can be on a personal level, a business level, or just friends or family getting out.

I continued to go to Montauk to check out the boats and the fish and find out what was coming in and what was the famous catch of the day. I would see the fishermen pulling out gigantic, gorgeous tuna, swordfish, or halibut, and there I was insisting on flukes, sea robins, blowfish, and whitebait. If I couldn't find them in Montauk, I looked for them in the fish markets of New York. But eventually I had to give up some of my preferred little friends from Tuscany and bring in those brash, arrogant fish that were so well represented on that part of the island.

By the end of July the tuna made their triumphal way to Sapore di mare. They broke through the front portals with all the arrogance of royalty. And they were accompanied by the applause of the kitchen staff.

T O N N O   I M P A Z Z A T O
T U N A   S W E A T E D   I N   T O M A T O E S
A N D   H E R B S

6 tablespoons / 90 ml olive oil
½ cup / 125 ml white wine
¼ teaspoon / 1 g crushed red
  pepper
Salt

2 garlic cloves, smashed
2 tablespoons / 24 g chopped
  parsley

Four 8-ounce / 240 g
  tuna steaks
6 plum tomatoes, peeled
  and chopped
¼ cup fresh chopped basil

Heat a large sauté pan over medium heat. Sauté the garlic in 4 tablespoons / 60 ml of the olive oil until it is golden. Add the tuna steaks and cook for 3 minutes on each side. Add the wine and red pepper and cook for about 1 minute, or until most of the liquid has evaporated. Add the tomatoes, cover, and cook for another 3 minutes. Uncover and add the herbs and salt to taste.

Place 1 tuna steak on each of 4 plates. With a slotted spoon, top each steak with a quarter of the tomato-herb mixture, leaving the liquid in the pan. Reduce the liquid by half, stirring constantly. Spoon the thickened sauce over the tuna and tomatoes. Drizzle with the remaining 2 tablespoons / 30 ml olive oil.

S E R V E S   4

CHAPTER 5

Mamma Goes Public

THERE ARE CUSTOMERS WHO WILL ALWAYS BE CUSTOMERS, CUSTOMERS WHO BECOME ACQUAINTANCES, AND CUSTOMERS WHO EVENTUALLY BECOME FRIENDS. I MET FRED PRESSMAN WHEN HE was a customer at my first restaurant, and our relationship developed quickly from understanding each other to having good feelings about one another. Then one day he asked me if I would like to open an Italian restaurant with him in a space he had found in New York's Chelsea neighborhood.

I have great respect for Fred, and I was excited about the idea of a new restaurant in Manhattan. Sapore di mare was a beautiful midsummer's dream, but I knew it would end the moment fall arrived. So returning to New York in the autumn of 1988 with the successful workings of Sapore in good hands, I looked forward to the possibility of a new project.

Out of the frying pan . . .

The joint venture with the Pressman family, Fred, Gene, and Bob, was established to continue the cultural crusade for Italian gastronomy in America. A gastronomical tradition has been transmitted through its leading character, the Italian mother. In honor of those who carry forth that tradition, I called the restaurant le Madri, "the mothers."

It was quite difficult in the beginning to get the press to understand that I wasn't talking about "mother" in the biblical sense. I was talking about the person who carries the burden for transmitting certain gastronomical memories, dishes, recipes that have always been in the family, whether she has children or not, is married or single. That's the way it is in Italy.

Le Madri blossomed in my mind. I wanted the interior to represent a certain period of Italian architecture, and the ceiling was my biggest challenge. I wanted a vaulted, scalloped ceiling, reminiscent of the lofty magnificence of sixteenth-century Italian architecture. It was successfully executed by a crew of ten Italian workers, and as they applied the stucco, I could imagine what it must have been like to build everything by hand, piece by piece, more than three hundred years ago.

Le Madri is an electrifying room combining a full-scale restaurant with a pizza oven and a pizza chef capable of using my little guys. Pizza with anchovies. Pizza with calamari. Pizza with scallops, clams, mussels.

It was exciting to put together a kitchen staff that was a crazy combination of talents and languages. At the beginning I hired an American-Italian chef, very young but a good person, very talented, with a great personality and great sensibility. Next to him I put three Italian women with varied culinary experiences. One was a single woman from Piedmont who had worked in restaurants a good part of her life. Another was a grandmother, who had been working with me for several years and brought with her a wealth of gastronomical wisdom from Rome. The third had been living in Brooklyn for twelve years and still had some memories of Italian cuisine and lots of experience as a home cook in this country. Placing these women alongside professional cooks and people who understand restaurants energized the kitchen and established a creative relationship between an American crew eager to learn and the standard-bearing mammas of Italian regional cooking. The head chef had the sensitivity to capture the quality of this relationship and make it work in a restaurant setting. We experimented daily with various menus and dishes, and most of the time everything blended perfectly.

I N S A L A T A   D I   C O Z Z E   E   Z U C C H I N I

S A L A D   O F   M U S S E L S   A N D
Z U C C H I N I

6 tablespoons/90 ml olive oil
¼ cup/60 ml white wine
Salt
Pepper

Juice of ½ lemon

2 pounds/1k mussels,
  shells rinsed and
  scraped clean
2 pounds/1k zucchini,
  julienned
8 leaves fresh mint,
  shredded

Heat 4 tablespoons/60 ml of the olive oil in a large sauté pan over high heat. Add the mussels and cook until the shells open. Discard any mussels that don't open. Add the white wine and simmer over medium heat until the wine evaporates. Remove the mussels from their shells, reserve the cooking liquid, and set aside.

Blanch the zucchini in salted water. Drain and set aside.

In a small bowl, whisk together the remaining 2 tablespoons/30 ml olive oil, the lemon juice, and 2 tablespoons/30 ml of the reserved cooking liquid. Add salt and pepper to taste.

Make a ring of zucchini around the edge of a serving platter. Pile the mussels in the center, sprinkle with mint, and drizzle with the dressing.

S E R V E S   4

Marta in action at
le Madri.

P A N I N O   C A L D O   A I   F R U T T I   D I   M A R E

W A R M   S E A F O O D   S A N D W I C H

Olive oil
Pinch of crushed red pepper
Salt

Juice of 1 lemon
1 tablespoon / 12 g minced
    parsley

2 baguettes or 4 rolls
¾ pound / 375 g clams,
    cleaned and scraped
¾ pound / 375 g mussels,
    cleaned and scraped
½ pound / 250 g razor
    clams, cleaned and
    scraped
½ pound / 250 g squid,
    bodies cut into rings

Cut the bread in half lengthwise, scoop out the soft center, and set aside in a mixing bowl. Toast the baguettes, cut each baguette in half crosswise, and set the bread aside.

Heat 3 tablespoons/45 ml olive oil in a large sauté pan over high heat. Add the crushed red pepper. Reduce the heat, add the shellfish and squid, and sauté until the shellfish open. Remove the seafood from the shells, discarding any shells that didn't open. Cut the razor clams into small pieces. In a bowl, toss the shellfish and squid together until they are well mixed.

Crumble the soft bread centers into a sauté pan coated with hot olive oil and sauté until golden brown. Add to the seafood mixture, drizzle with olive oil and lemon juice, add the parsley, and toss well. Taste for salt.

Pile the mixture onto the 4 baguettes, close the sandwiches, and serve.

S E R V E S   4

Aren't we beautiful?

I GREW UP A GOOD Italian boy. Even though I am reaching the age of forty, I still feel that I need an Italian mother figure around when I want to have a conversation about food. An Italian mother is someone you can fall back on when you really want to eat, when you want to recall certain gastronomical memories related to home, friends, and familiar dishes, and I was re-creating this familiar situation around me at le Madri. In my other restaurants I was the mentor. Now there was a real exchange that brought back flavors I had forgotten. So I was happy to see my chefs and *le Madri* coming up with things I could hardly remember myself. It was the groundbreaker for a more detailed and original menu, and I was getting closer to what I was reaching for.

We started to do squash blossoms with anchovies and ricotta cheese and mozzarella; we created a sauce that was made out of Sicilian ingredients such as black olives, tomatoes, capers, and anchovies. We featured sardines that were butterflied, filleted, and poached with onions in wine; cuttlefish with its ink found its way into risotto and pasta. We were working with red mullet, filleted and poached ("sweated," as we say in Italy) in a very light tomato sauce with wine. We started to bring in an abundance of really great fish from Italy: sea breams, *spigola*, and eels, the small-to-medium guys from the Mediterranean, which we stuffed with rosemary, seasoned with salt and pepper, and lightly broiled until the skin was crisp.

S P I E D I N I   D I   A N G U I L L E
G R I L L E D   S K E W E R S   O F   E E L

Bay leaves
Salt
Pepper

Lemon peel, cut into 1-inch/
 3-cm pieces
Shallots, peeled

2 pounds / 1k medium eels

Using a wooden skewer, spear a piece of eel, a bay leaf, a piece of lemon peel, and a whole shallot. Repeat the sequence until 4 skewers are full (leave an inch at each end of the skewer so you can grab it). Sprinkle with salt and pepper and place the skewers on a heated grill. Cook until the eel is tender but still moist, about 4 to 5 minutes.

S E R V E S   4

O R A T A   A R R O S T O   C O N   E R B E   A R O M A T I C H E
O R A T A   B A K E D   W I T H   A R O M A T I C   H E R B S

Orata is a Mediterranean fish in the sea-bream family.

Salt

Pepper

½ cup / 125 ml olive oil

½ cup / 125 ml white wine

½ cup / 125 ml concentrated fish or clam broth

4 whole 1-pound / 500-g sea breams, cleaned and scaled

1 rosemary sprig

Fresh thyme, sage, and tarragon

Heat the oven to 400°F/200°C. Salt and pepper the fish well inside and out. Heat the olive oil in a large ovenproof sauté pan (use a pan large enough to hold all the fish flat). Lay the sea breams in the hot oil and brown on both sides over medium-high heat. Place the pan in the oven and bake the fish for about 5 minutes. Remove from the oven, and pour the white wine evenly over all the fish. Cook over high heat until the wine reduces. Pour the broth over the fish; place it in the oven for 6 to 7 more minutes. When the flesh is firm, transfer the fish to individual serving dishes, sprinkle with herbs, drizzle with pan juices, and serve.

S E R V E S   4

AS WEIRD AS IT SOUNDS, I cherished my secret relationship with the fish that were flown in from Italy once a week. They used to arrive early in the morning, well packed, nice and fresh, all lined up, their beautiful, vivid eyes wide open, standing up with their nice, cutesy bodies—and they were always put in the worst part of the cooling box. They were never dressed up right away; they were taken into consideration a little later, unlike the tuna, swordfish, and snapper that came in every day with the same arrogant attitude, demanding immediate personal attention.

One day I decided that I had to put my foot down. I told my staff that if they shoveled my Italian ambassadors into the back of the walk-in box it was probably because that's where they were in their heads. "When the Italians come," I said sternly, "I want to see them prepared, set up, put in their places ready to go at the same time as the tuna and swordfish." I was making a statement about prejudice to my American staff. I wanted these guys taken care of with the best. They were of the freshest and best quality, and I needed support from the kitchen if they were to be appreciated in the dining room.

I am very pleased to say that we serve them now at le Madri consistently. Unfortunately, the mackerel is not appreciated as much as some other guys, but it is one of my personal favorites.

One evening six or seven months into the success of le Madri I was making my routine check. I'm the kind of restaurateur who treats his restaurant like his own house; every corner of the place is checked, inspected, used, and lived in. Walking downstairs after the normal hour of service, I saw some of the dishwashers cleaning up, and I was disturbed by one of the cleaning crew's grumbling in Spanish. I asked him what was wrong. He showed me a linen napkin containing the remains of one of the night's fish specials. I knew what we had served that night; it had to be one of my beautiful *bronzini* or *spigola* from Italy. What was going on here? How could someone eat only part of such a fish, so delicate, so light, and then abandon it to the wastebasket? I had to find out how many other people were doing this.

Two weeks later I was told that almost every night a linen napkin

Clams in transit.

with food in it was found in the ladies' room wastebasket, and nine times out of ten it contained one of the fish specials. I had customers coming to my restaurant who said they loved my food and then threw it into the wastebasket. There was something seriously wrong.

I called a meeting with the wait staff and told them to be very kind and very discreet but to observe the customers from their stations and bring to my attention anyone engaging in this strange behavior. It was not a question of confronting the culprit, but just to consider taking a different direction in regard to my fish specialties of the house before they became the specialties of the garbage.

Another week went by, and finally the waiters called to my attention two very good customers who came three or four nights a week. I asked myself how I was going to approach the problem.

I went over to the table and said, "Tonight we're not going to have the usual specials here." I didn't mention the cuttlefish, the red mullet, whatever dish was the belle of the night. I kept myself focused on vegetables and pastas. To my surprise the lady in question asked what the fish specials were. I reluctantly mentioned the *orate* flown in fresh from Italy, and she ordered it. I must have looked surprised because she said, "I always like to order the fish that you feature as specialties because they have the most interesting taste. They are never boring."

That night we found the remains of the little fish in a napkin downstairs in the ladies' room wastebasket. At least I got some comfort in knowing that although one of my best customers may have had an eating problem, she was not prejudiced against Italian fish. Since then I have vetoed anyone's checking the wastebaskets. There is no need for me to follow the itinerary of my fish beyond the kitchen. As long as my customers like the taste of my fish, they don't even have to swallow it.

P E S C I O L I N I   F R I T T I
F R I E D   W H I T I N G

Salt
Pepper
Vegetable oil
All-purpose flour

¼ cup / 60 ml milk
8 parsley sprigs, coarsely
chopped

4 large whiting fillets
(10 to 12 inches / 25 to
30 cm each), cut into
1-inch / 3-cm pieces

Sprinkle the whiting with salt and pepper. Place the fish in a bowl and pour in the milk.

Heat the oil in a large frying pan (or deep-fat fryer) over medium heat. Dredge the whiting in flour, shake off the excess, and fry until golden brown. Drain on paper towels. Sprinkle with salt and parsley and serve hot.

S E R V E S   4

M E R L U Z Z O   a l l '   A G R O
M A C K E R E L   W I T H   O I L   A N D   L E M O N

½ cup / 125 ml white wine
6 black peppercorns
1 bay leaf
¼ cup / 60 ml olive oil
Salt and pepper

2 whole parsley sprigs
Juice of 1 lemon
2 parsley sprigs, coarsely
chopped

4 fresh whole mackerel
(12 inches / 30 cm
each), cleaned and
gutted, with heads and
tails removed

In a shallow saucepan bring the wine, ¼ cup/60 ml water, peppercorns, bay leaf, and whole parsley sprigs to a boil. Add the fish, cover, reduce heat, and simmer until the fish is cooked.

Remove the fish from the broth. Fillet them and place them on a platter. Sprinkle with the olive oil, lemon juice, salt and pepper to taste, and chopped parsley. Serve hot or at room temperature.

S E R V E S   4

M E R L U Z Z O   I N   P A D E L L A
C O N   P E P E R O N I

M A C K E R E L   S A U T É E D   W I T H   S W E E T
P E P P E R S

1 tablespoon / 15 ml olive oil
1 cup / 250 ml white wine
Salt
Pepper
1 teaspoon / 4 g capers, rinsed

2 celery stalks, julienned
1 red onion, sliced

1 red bell pepper,
  julienned
1 green bell pepper,
  julienned
1 yellow bell pepper,
  julienned
4 fresh mackerel fillets
  (6 to 8 ounces / 180
  to 240 g each)
20 basil leaves, torn

Heat the olive oil in a medium sauté pan. Sauté the celery and onion until soft. Add the white wine and reduce slightly. Add the peppers and ½ cup/125 ml water, cover, and braise gently for 7 to 8 minutes to soften the peppers. Remove the lid and lay the fish over the vegetables. Sprinkle with salt and pepper, add the capers and more water if the vegetables are dry, cover again, and cook for 5 minutes, or until the mackerel is done. Transfer to a serving platter, top with the basil leaves, and serve.

S E R V E S   4

Let's run faster.

The Coco Pazzo Dance

F

INALLY I WAS READY TO MAKE MY BIG DEBUT ON NEW YORK'S UPPER EAST SIDE. BUT WAS THE UPPER EAST SIDE READY FOR PINO FROM ITALY AND MARK FROM QUEENS? MARK HAD BEEN KEPT IN quarantine for more than three years at Sapore di mare, and although he was happy enough in the summer, he missed the action of the city in the winter. I told him he had paid his dues in East Hampton and brought him back into New York again.

So . . . here we come into one of the most conservative, wealthy neighborhoods in the city. We just barged in with nice smiles on our faces that said "Here we are. I know we might not belong here, but if you're looking for a neighborhood place with some real food, we're here to make you happy."

I can still see the scene. Me, tall and heavyset. Mark, short and definitely heavyset. Both bringing sustenance to this classy neighborhood where everything was so perfect—and so empty. But we were received with enthusiasm, so we must have been doing something right.

Coco in Tuscan means "cook"; *pazzo* means "crazy," crazy about the freedom to cook without rules. Coco Pazzo offers the quintessential expression of post–peasant food in an urban environment. It fits my definition of freedom because it doesn't commit us to specific concepts, rules, or menu planning. Appetizers that would be listed as appetizers in the most traditional regional menu we turn into main courses at lunch. We serve *cacciucco*, the gutsy Tuscan fish stew, in large bowls and turn it into a family sharing experience. We give Tuscan food a touch of theatricality that has been missing.

S P I G O L A   A L   F O R N O
R O A S T E D   B A B Y   B L A C K   B A S S   W I T H   O L I V E S   A N D   O R E G A N O

You could substitute grouper or striped bass here.

Salt
Pepper
2 tablespoons/30 ml extra
   virgin olive oil
2 cups/500 ml white wine
¼ pound/125 g black olives,
   pitted

4 garlic cloves, peeled

4 black bass, about
   1 pound/500 g each
2 rosemary sprigs, chopped
1 bunch oregano

Have the fishmonger clean the fish and remove all the scales.

Preheat the oven to 475°F/240°C. Open the fish cavity and sprinkle liberally with salt. Stuff with the herbs and garlic and place the fish in a well-oiled roasting pan. Sprinkle the skin of the fish with salt and pepper to taste, drizzle with the olive oil and the white wine.

Place the fish in the oven and roast for about 10 minutes per pound/500 g. When the fish is cooked, there should be no blood coming from the cavity. Two minutes before the fish should be done, sprinkle the olives around it and let it cook for the remaining time. Add more wine to the roasting pan if it starts to dry during cooking. Remove the fish from the pan with a spatula and serve whole on a platter. Pour the juices from the pan over the fish.

S E R V E S   4

I take it into the dining room.

B R A N Z I N I   I N   C A R T O C C I O
S T R I P E D   B A S S   B A K E D   I N   P A R C H M E N T

*4 large pieces of parchment
   (12 by 12 inches / 30 by
   30 cm each)*
Salt
Pepper
½ cup / 125 ml olive oil
½ cup / 125 ml white wine

2 lemons

*4 striped bass fillets
   (8 ounces / 250 g each)*
8 rosemary sprigs
4 oregano sprigs

Preheat the oven to 400°F/200°C.

Slice the lemons into ¼-inch-thick wheels and place a few on each of the pieces of parchment. Place a fillet on each and season with salt and pepper to taste. Fold the sides of each packet up so they create a wall on each side of the fillet. Drizzle 2 tablespoons/30 ml of the olive oil and of the white wine over each fillet. Lay the sprigs of herbs over the fish and fold the pouches closed at the top (fold so that you can easily open the pouches to check the fish for doneness). Place the pouches on a baking sheet and bake for 5 to 10 minutes, depending on the thickness of the fish (check for doneness after 5 minutes). The fish is cooked when the flesh is slightly firm and the herbs and lemons are discolored. To serve, open the packets in front of the guests.

S E R V E S   4

N E W   Y O R K E R S   H A V E   T O   L E A R N how to relax, and I am trying to get them to do so more and more. There are places where the scenes are and where people gather to be seen. The press labels certain restaurants "in" and certain restaurants "out"; there are the must-be-seen-in restaurants, the must-go-to restaurants, and the if-you-miss-it-you're-a-jerk restaurants. We decided to be a restaurant where you go to

relax and have fun. It turns out there was not a better area to choose than the Upper East Side.

The dining table is a great leveler, and we are all equal when we sit down to it. It's wonderful to see a party with three or four people having fun over a big bowl of *cacciucco*. Although at the beginning there were people who resisted it, we now have a fully developed clientele who come regularly on the nights we have our family-style menu.

Where is the fish?

P O L P O   A L L A   G R I G L I A
G R I L L E D   O C T O P U S

6 tablespoons/90 ml olive oil
2 tablespoons/30 ml red wine
   vinegar
Crushed red pepper
Dried oregano
Salt

2 garlic cloves, crushed
1 red onion, sliced

2 pounds/1 k fresh
   octopus, cleaned

The octopus must be boiled to tenderize it before you marinate it. Place the whole octopus bodies in boiling, unsalted water for 30 to 40 minutes, or until tender. Remove the octopus from the water and let it cool.

Cut the octopus bodies in half, or in quarters if you prefer. Place the octopus in a bowl and add the oil, vinegar, garlic, and onion. Season with the red pepper, oregano, and salt to taste. Toss well, cover, and let marinate for 24 to 36 hours in the refrigerator.

One hour before grilling, remove the octopus from the refrigerator to bring it to room temperature. Take the octopus out of the marinade, saving the liquid to dress the grilled octopus. Sprinkle the octopus with more dried oregano and grill until crunchy. To serve, place on a platter and sauce with the reserved marinade. This dish can be served hot or at room temperature.

S E R V E S   6

I N S A L A T A   D I   C O Z Z E   E   P A T A T E

M U S S E L   A N D   P O T A T O   S A L A D

¼ cup/60 ml plus 3 table-
spoons/45 ml olive oil
1 cup/250 ml white wine
Salt
Pepper

8 new potatoes, scrubbed
2 garlic cloves, smashed
½ carrot, diced
1 celery stalk, diced
1 small onion, diced
1 tablespoon/15 ml lemon juice

3 dozen mussels, cleaned
8 basil leaves, torn

Cook the potatoes in a large pot of boiling salted water. When they are fork tender, remove them from the water and let them cool.

Brown the garlic in ¼ cup/60 ml olive oil in a large sauté pan. Add the carrot, celery, and onion and sauté for a minute, then add the mussels and white wine, and simmer gently until all the mussels have opened. Discard any mussels that remain closed. Let the mussels cool to room temperature, then remove them from their shells. Slice the cooled potatoes into 1-inch/3-cm cubes. Place the mussels and potatoes in a large bowl. Season with salt and pepper to taste, add the basil, and drizzle with 3 tablespoons/45 ml of the olive oil and the lemon juice. Toss so that the salad is well covered with the dressing, but not so vigorously that the potatoes break up. Serve at room temperature.

S E R V E S   4

C O C O   P A Z Z O   I S   T H E   R E S U L T of a social-gastronomical experiment. It allowed me to really understand how all New Yorkers, even on the Upper East Side, long to be part of this huge melting pot, and not just an overflow of humanity watching from the sidelines. I have to say Coco Pazzo has worked very well and is still working well. I like to think that in a certain way it has changed the restaurant scene, and I guess the *New York Times* agreed when they called it the best restaurant to open in New York City in 1990.

The success of sardines and anchovies on Seventy-fourth and Madison deserves an announcement. They are finally making their way into the mouths of adoring customers, and it happened in a very smooth and painless way in authentic, Tuscan style.

I N S A L A T A   D I   S A R D E   F R E S C H E   E   V E G E T A L I

W A R M   F R E S H   S A R D I N E   S A L A D   W I T H   S U M M E R   V E G E T A B L E S

Flour

2 tablespoons/30 ml vegetable oil

6 tablespoons/90 ml extra virgin olive oil

10 capers

10 black olives, pitted

Salt and pepper

2 tablespoons/30 ml red wine vinegar

4 russet potatoes

1 garlic clove, smashed

1 bunch arugula

1 head curly endive

¼ cup/48 g hulled fresh peas

¼ pound/125 g sugar snap peas

24 fresh sardine fillets

3 plum tomatoes, diced

Wash and dry the salad greens. Divide them evenly on 4 dinner plates and set them aside.

Boil the potatoes. Let them cool, then peel them and cut them into cubes. Blanch the fresh peas and clean the sugar snaps.

Dredge the sardines in flour, and sauté them in the vegetable oil in a large frying pan. Remove from the pan and place on paper towels to drain. Wipe out the frying pan, then pour in the olive oil and add both kinds of peas, the potatoes, tomatoes, capers, garlic, and olives. Sauté for 1 or 2 minutes. When the sugar snap peas have wilted, return the sardines to the pan and season with salt and pepper to taste and the red wine vinegar. Sauté for 30 seconds more. Spoon over the salad greens and serve immediately.

S E R V E S   4

CHAPTER 7

Chefs Talk

Pino:

When I first came to New York, working in a restaurant was the only way I could make a living while I was learning the language. I was having fun dealing with people and dealing with food, but after a while I felt that being a chef was a limitation and that it would be more satisfying to be in on all ends of the business. So I decided to become a restaurateur. Now you guys are all chefs. Why did you become chefs? Or maybe you want to be restaurateurs. Marta, you did own a restaurant in Italy and decided to become a chef in New York? I think I know the answer for you, Mark. You like to travel.

Mark:

Yeah. I've always liked to travel ever since I was a kid. My friends and I used to go to the Cape in the summer and eat steamers and clams on the half shell.

Pino:

I have always thought it was because you just wanted to get out of Queens.

Mark:

Maybe, but I also love to cook, although I didn't suddenly decide I wanted to be a chef. I have always worked in the food business. The first job I had was selling peanuts in Shea Stadium when I was fourteen. Then I graduated to hot dogs, soda, and ice cream.

Pino:

Marta, why did you want to become a chef?

Marta:

It is a very creative profession, and every day it changes. I have always loved to cook. I started cooking with my mother when I was ten or twelve years old. And when I was older I began to cook to catch my husband. Then after we were married I cooked for my sons and my friends. My friends enjoyed my cooking so much that they always preferred coming to my house to going to a restaurant. When I opened my own restaurant, they kept coming to my restaurant just as they had come to my house.

I'll cook it all.

Mark:

Marta, you say you learned to cook to get a husband. I used to cook to attract girlfriends. I thought the way to a woman's heart was through her stomach. And most of the time I was right.

Now my wife cooks at home. She wants to learn, and she's a good cook. Most men view cooking as a hobby like tennis or golf or a barbecue on Saturday night. They cook if they feel like it. Women are usually the ones who make breakfast, lunch, and dinner for the family.

Marta:

In the local dialect of Emilia-Romagna the woman who takes care of the house is called *rezdora; rezdora* means "the woman who rules the house." In Emilia the women are very versatile; they are the administrators of the household, and it is a term of great respect.

• • • A B O U T   M A R K E T S

Marta:

I love to go to the market. I used to go every day when I had my restaurant in Modena. In Modena the market is in the middle of the old city. There are many different carts with vegetables and fruits, meat, and fish, and the vendors speak their local dialect. I would pick out the freshest things and then plan my menu from that. I don't like to go as much here, but I need to have the experience of going so I can see what is available and plan what to cook the next day.

Mark:

Shopping for the restaurant here we depend on our purchasing agent, but I call the purveyors to find out what's good and go to the markets in New York at least once a week for inspiration.

· · · · A B O U T   R E S T A U R A N T S

Mark:

When you go into a restaurant in Italy there is an energy and enthusiasm associated with the food. There are families, things are moving, people are walking around. This energy and enthusiasm are a result of loving what you're doing in the kitchen. That's what Pino brought to America besides Tuscan cooking. I think it has to do with wanting to please people, to take care of them in a special way.

Marta:

Of course. Once a psychologist told me that cooking was like nursing a baby. It is a form of nurturing.

Mark:

When you go to a restaurant and you ask for something special, maybe sauce on the side or something out of the ordinary, and the chef comes back with, "I can't do that," it's probably not someone who loves what he or she does. The restaurant business is part of the hospitality industry, and you have to live up to that if you want to have satisfied customers.

· · · A N D   C U S T O M E R S

Marta:

There is a man that comes into le Madri who I've come to know by name because he always asks for salt and sauce on the side. I'll say to the waiter, "Ah, Mr. ——— must be here tonight."

Mark:

We have a customer at Coco Pazzo who we named a salad after. She likes it with beans, lentils, and tomato chopped up very fine.

Giving customers what they want is what makes a restaurant great. For example, if we don't have *spaghetti vongole* on the menu, a lot of customers know I'll make it special for them. They may have all the money in the world, but it only works for them when they are treated in a special way.

Marta:

People want to be treated special. When a man comes in with a beautiful woman, he wants to impress her; he wants to look good in her eyes; he wants her to see that everyone knows him. "Look how important I am, everybody is doing things for me." One customer I know always sends back the wine when he is with a woman, saying that the wine is corky. When the same man comes in alone, or with another man the wine is fine.

Mark:

In a sense, every restaurant has to operate like a friendly, neighborhood restaurant to survive. New York is big. There are eight million people. How many Modenas with two hundred thousand people are there in New York?

Marta:

Many of our customers live in the neighborhood, and they come in several times a week. We have one customer who comes every day, and he never wants what's on the menu. I try to give him what he wants but sometimes it's impossible.

Mark:

Yes, it is. I'll buy a whole tuna, and when I slice it, of course, not each piece is exactly the same; it doesn't come out of a six-ounce can, it comes out of the ocean. It's hard to convince customers that we don't fish it, we don't grow it, we just cook what nature gave us.

Marta:

We try to make the portions all the same size, but sometimes it's hard to get each plate exactly the same. Once I served two salads at the same table, and one plate had a few more leaves of lettuce than the other; it came back with a request for more leaves. And two or three days ago a customer told me that she wanted lobster, but she didn't want to see the shell!

Mark:

The world is full of idiosyncrasies, and people have peculiar hang-ups about food.

Marta:

I like to suggest fish like sardines, anchovies, and whiting until people become familiar with it and start to ask for it. This year it is doing much better than last.

Get me the waiter who wrote this order.

. . . A B O U T   F I S H

Marta:

Fish is a big seller at le Madri, especially in the summertime.

Mark:

And especially in New York, where people are so health conscious.

Marta:

Fish, lamb, and veal, in that order, are the most popular dishes at le Madri. We sell a lot of steak, but fish is our biggest seller. People mostly ask for tuna, swordfish, snapper. But the mackerel, shad, sardines, and anchovies move as well.

Mark:

And they're available from every country all year.

Codfish is a forgotten fish for sure. I like to stew it Livornese style with tomatoes, olives, capers, fresh tomatoes, and oregano. No one really knows what codfish is, but the Northeast grew up eating it. Any white-fish was called cod.

I N S A L A T A   D I   B A C C A L À   F R E D D O   C O N   S A L S A   V E R D E
P O A C H E D   C O D   W I T H   C U C U M B E R S   A N D   G R E E N   S A U C E

1 tablespoon / 15 ml red wine
  vinegar
2 tablespoons / 30 ml olive oil
Salt
Pepper
4 tablespoons / 160 m white
  wine or vinegar
2 bay leaves
2 cloves
6 black peppercorns

2 onions
1 parsley sprig

2 cucumbers
Four 6-ounce / 180 g
  fresh cod fillets
Fresh dill

FOR THE GREEN SAUCE

8 cornichons

½ cup/125 ml extra virgin
   olive oil

Dash of Worcestershire

1 bunch parsley

1 bunch basil

1 marjoram sprig

1 rosemary sprig

1 thyme sprig

1 egg, hard-cooked and peeled

Juice of 1 lemon

Peel and seed the cucumbers and slice them very thin. Peel one of the onions and slice it paper thin. Mix these together and dress with red wine vinegar, olive oil, and salt and pepper to taste. Cool in the refrigerator.

To poach the fish, place the fillets in a large pot or deep roasting pan and cover them with water. Pour in the wine or vinegar. Peel the remaining onion and stick the bay leaves to it with the cloves. Place the onion, peppercorns, and parsley in the liquid and start to simmer slowly. The fish will take 5 to 10 minutes to cook, depending on its thickness. Test the cod after 5 minutes—the fish is done when the flesh is firm, but not hard. Remove the fish from the broth and chill. If you are cooking the fish ahead of time, store the fish in its own broth.

To make the green sauce, place the herbs, cornichons, and hard-cooked egg in a food processor and chop very fine. Mix very well with the lemon juice, olive oil, and Worcestershire sauce. Cool the sauce in the refrigerator.

To serve, line each dinner plate with the green sauce, place some cucumber salad in the center, and place a piece of cod over the cucumbers. Garnish with fresh dill. The fish can be served hot or cold.

SERVES 4

BACCALÀ CON SALSA AI CAPPERI

FRESH COD WITH CAPERS

FOR THE BROTH

1 cinnamon stick

Several whole black peppercorns

2 cups / 500 ml white wine vinegar

Salt

2 garlic cloves

1 onion, quartered

1 carrot, cut into ½-inch / 1-cm pieces

1 celery stalk, cut into ½-inch / 1-cm pieces

½ lemon

One 2-pound / 1-k whole fresh cod, cleaned and scaled

FOR THE SAUCE

⅓ cup / 83 ml olive oil

2 anchovies, preserved in salt, rinsed

1 tablespoon / 12 g capers, finely chopped

2 garlic cloves, smashed

3 shallots, minced

1 small parsley sprig, finely chopped

½ small yellow bell pepper, roasted, seeded, and cut into slivers (see page 113)

To make the broth, put all the ingredients except the fish in a large pot with 2 quarts/2 l water and boil for 15 minutes. Add the cod and simmer for about 5 minutes, until firm. Remove the pot from the heat and place it in cold water to cool slightly. Fillet the fish while it is still warm and set it aside in a deep, covered serving dish.

To make the sauce, sauté the garlic in olive oil until golden, then remove it from the pan. Add the anchovies and let them melt in the oil. Add the bell pepper, shallots, capers, and parsley and sauté for about 5 minutes, until the flavors are combined. Pour the sauce over the fish and serve warm.

SERVES 4

. . . A B O U T   S P A G H E T T I   A L L A   P E S C A T O R A

Marta:

There are a million ways to make *spaghetti alla pescatora.* The way I love to make it best is just with clams, garlic, and parsley cooked in white wine so you can still taste the sea.

Mark:

I use a combination of octopus, squid, mussels, clams, and sometimes add shrimp and scallops to it.

S P A G H E T T I   A L L A   P E S C A T O R A
F I S H E R M A N ' S   P A S T A ,   M A R K ' S   S T Y L E

1 pound / 500 g spaghetti
¼ cup / 60 ml extra virgin
   olive oil
Pinch of crushed red pepper
Salt
½ cup / 125 ml canned whole
   tomatoes
½ cup / 125 ml white wine

2 garlic cloves, sliced
1 teaspoon / 4 g chopped parsley

1 pound / 500 g calamari,
   cleaned
½ pound / 250 g cooked
   octopus
1 teaspoon / 4 g fresh
   chopped basil
1 teaspoon / 4 g fresh
   chopped oregano
8 clams, cleaned and
   scrubbed
12 mussels, cleaned and
   scrubbed

Place a large pot of salted water over high heat to boil for the pasta. In a large sauté pan brown the garlic in the olive oil. When the garlic is golden brown, add the calamari and the octopus. Sauté for a few moments, then add a sprinkle of crushed red pepper, salt, the fresh herbs, clams, mussels, tomatoes, and white wine. Simmer slowly until the shells open. Discard any shellfish that don't open. If the sauce is still watery at this point, continue cooking until it has thickened slightly.

Add the spaghetti to the boiling water and cook until al dente. Drain the pasta, saving a cup of the pasta water. Add the pasta to the sauce and toss until all the pasta is coated. If the sauce is too thick, add a spoonful or two of the pasta water. Serve the pasta on a large platter, arranging the clams and mussels around the edge of the platter. Serve immediately.

S E R V E S   4

. . . A B O U T   C A L A M A R I

Mark:

I also make a *calamari pescatora* which is just calamari stewed down with white wine and tomatoes, a little bit of herbs, a little crushed red pepper, and served on soft polenta with peas. You have to cook calamari for thirty or thirty-five minutes so it's nice and tender and it lets off a lot of liquid, which has so much flavor.

Most people who eat calamari like it fried, but I think the best way to eat it is stewed. Fried it is a fun finger food, but if you stew it you get all the flavor, and all the nutrients are still in the broth.

Bye, bye . . . Coco's last touch.

C A L A M A R I   A L L A   P E S C A T O R A
S T U F F E D   C A L A M A R I , F I S H E R M A N ' S   S T Y L E

2 anchovy fillets, preserved
  in salt or oil, rinsed
Salt
Pepper
2 tablespoons / 24 g bread
  crumbs
Pinch of nutmeg
2 tablespoons / 30 ml olive oil
4 tablespoons / 60 ml white
  wine
½ cup / 125 ml canned whole
  tomatoes, milled
1 teaspoon / 4 g dried oregano

1 garlic clove, chopped
4 tablespoons / 60 ml heavy
  cream
1 egg yolk
1 tablespoon / 12 g grated
  Parmesan
2 tablespoons / 24 g minced
  onion
1 small garlic clove, minced

12 medium calamari
  bodies, cleaned, tentacles
  separated
⅓ pound / 166 g halibut
  or other whitefish,
  filleted
¼ pound / 125 g sea
  scallops
¼ pound / 125 g shrimp,
  peeled and deveined
2 thyme sprigs
2 rosemary sprigs
2 tablespoons / 24 g fresh
  peas

Blanch the calamari bodies and tentacles in boiling water for 2 minutes, until they shrink lightly. Remove them from the water and let them cool.

In a food processor, grind the garlic, halibut, scallops, shrimp, and anchovy fillets until smooth. Add the heavy cream, egg yolk, Parmesan, salt, and pepper and process until the mixture is smooth. Add the bread crumbs, nutmeg, and herbs and mix well. Place in the refrigerator to cool.

Fill the calamari bodies ¾ full with the seafood mixture. Do not overfill, as the mixture expands when it cooks. "Stitch" the bodies closed with a toothpick.

In a large sauté pan, brown the onion and garlic in olive oil. Add the calamari bodies and tentacles, white wine, tomatoes, and oregano and simmer over medium heat until the tomatoes are cooked, about 20 minutes. Add the peas about 4 minutes before the sauce is finished. Remove the toothpicks from the calamari and serve immediately.

S E R V E S   6

POLPETTI AFFOGATI
DROWNED BABY OCTOPUS

2 or 3 tablespoons / 30 or 45 ml olive oil

1 tablespoon / 12 g Kalamata olives, pitted

1 teaspoon / 4 g salted capers, rinsed

2 garlic cloves, smashed

1 teaspoon / 4 g chopped parsley

1 pound / 500 g fresh baby octopus, cleaned

Generous pinch of fresh rosemary

2 tomatoes, peeled and diced

1 small hot pepper, minced (optional)

In a medium saucepan, heat the oil over medium heat. Add the octopus, olives, capers, rosemary, garlic, and tomatoes. Cover and simmer over low heat for about 30 minutes. Stir occasionally to make sure the octopus isn't sticking to the bottom of the pan. If necessary, add water a little at a time so it doesn't dry out. Before serving, add the fresh parsley and a pinch of the hot pepper if desired. Toss gently and serve hot.

SERVES 4

Mark:

Octopus is the most misunderstood food in the world. People think they don't want to eat it because of the tentacles, but I don't think I've ever served octopus to anyone who didn't like it once they got up the courage to eat it.

. . . AND ABOUT CACCIUCCO

Mark:

Basically there are two ways to cook: country-style and haute cuisine—peasant and bourgeois. Nowhere is this more evident than in the variety of *cacciucco*, the fish stews, of Tuscany.

Marta:

Cacciucco comes from fishing villages where you had fish *alla griglia* on Monday, poached fish on Tuesday, and by Thursday and Friday you were looking for a different flavor.

Cacciucco is a whole meal. You have the broth, the fish, and the bread. You put bread in the bottom of the bowl to soak up the broth. All the leftovers would be used, all the small, usually inexpensive Mediterranean fish with lots of bones. Here you can use monkfish, and other inexpensive fish.

C A C C I U C C O   A L L A   T O S C A N A
T U S C A N   S E A F O O D   S T E W

¼ cup / 60 ml extra virgin
   olive oil
Pinch of crushed red pepper
2 cups / 500 ml white wine
¾ cup / 188 ml canned
   tomatoes
Salt

2 garlic cloves, sliced
1 onion, thinly sliced
1½ cups / 375 ml fish stock
   (see page 121)
1 tablespoon / 12 g chopped
   parsley, plus additional
   for serving

½ pound / 250 g octopus,
   cleaned
3 pounds / 1,5 k calamari,
   cleaned
¾ pound / 375 g monkfish
24 mussels, cleaned and
   scrubbed
24 clams, cleaned and
   scrubbed
1 tablespoon / 12 g fresh
   rosemary
1 tablespoon / 12 g fresh
   oregano
18 scallops
18 medium shrimp, peeled

F O R   T H E   G A R L I C   B R E A D

2 tablespoons / 30 ml oil

6 garlic cloves, peeled

12 slices good Italian bread, preferably 1-day old

Place the octopus in boiling, unsalted water and cook for 40 minutes, or until tender. Remove the octopus from the water, cool, and cut into 1-inch/3-cm pieces. Cut the cleaned calamari into rings and the monkfish into 1-inch/3-cm pieces.

In a large soup pot, brown the garlic in the olive oil over medium heat. Add the calamari, crushed red pepper, and onion and cook until the onion is soft. Add the octopus, mussels, clams, white wine, tomatoes, herbs, and fish stock. Turn down the heat and let the soup simmer slowly until the shellfish have opened and the tomatoes have cooked into the broth. Discard any shells that don't open.

Add the monkfish and simmer for 1 minute. Add the scallops and simmer for another minute. Add the shrimp and cook for about 3 more minutes, until the shrimp are done. Taste for salt. Remove the stew from the heat immediately. Place a piece of garlic bread in the bottom of individual bowls and slowly ladle the soup over the bread, being careful not to break up the pieces of fish. Garnish with chopped parsley and a drizzle of extra virgin olive oil. Serve additional pieces of garlic bread on the side.

To make the garlic bread, toast the bread slices and scrape a clove of garlic over 1 side of each slice until the clove disintegrates. Drizzle the bread with olive oil.

S E R V E S   6

Hot plate!

BRODETTO ALLA PESCATORA

FISH SOUP, FISHERMAN'S STYLE

Brodetto alla Pescatora, cousin to the heartier cacciucco, *is a traditional dish found on the Adriatic coast. More of a fish soup, it is a lighter, less spicy version of the traditional* cacciucco *stew.*

FOR THE FISH BROTH

1 celery stalk, cut into
  ½-inch / 1-cm pieces
1 carrot, cut into ½-inch /
  1-cm pieces
1 onion, halved

Fish heads and tails
  (reserved from fish for
  the soup)

FOR THE SOUP

½ cup / 125 ml olive oil
½ cup / 125 ml white wine
1 tablespoon / 15 ml white
  wine vinegar
Salt
Pepper

1 onion, roughly chopped
2 garlic cloves, sliced
1 teaspoon / 4 g chopped parsley

1 pound / 500 g fresh
  tomatoes, peeled and
  pureed
2 pounds mixed mussels
  and Manila clams, in
  the shells
1 pound / 500 g mixed
  fish, including cuttlefish,
  squid, red mullet, and
  monkfish, cleaned, boned,
  and cut into chunks
  (save the heads and tails
  for the broth)
4 slices country bread,
  toasted

To make the broth, put the celery, carrot, and onion in a large stockpot with 3 quarts water and heat until boiling. Add the fish heads and tails and simmer for 30 minutes. Reserve.

To make the soup, sauté the chopped onion and sliced garlic in the olive oil until golden. Remove the garlic from the pan and discard. Pour in the white wine and reduce slightly. Add the tomatoes, vinegar, and salt and pepper to taste and simmer for about 5 minutes, stirring occasionally. Add the mussels, clams, cuttlefish, and squid and a ladle of the fish broth. Cook for 5 minutes, then add the other fish, starting with the largest pieces. The clams and mussels should be open; discard any that are still closed. While the fish is cooking, add the rest of the broth, a ladleful at a time. Cook for about 10 more minutes, then gently mix in the parsley.

To serve, place a piece of toasted bread on the bottom of each bowl, and ladle the soup and an assortment of fish over the bread.

S E R V E S   4

Mark:

Whiting is good to put in *cacciucco*. I use mussels, clams, octopus, squid, and any other pieces of fish I have around.

Marta:

In many places the most unfancy fish is passed through the food mill to extract the juice and make a pulp so there is a thick broth; very tasty, of course. But then others prefer a lighter, clearer broth, and in that case you would use wine and tomatoes.

COZZE E VONGOLE IN BRODETTO

CLAM AND MUSSEL SOUP

1 cup/250 ml white wine
8 tablespoons/120 ml olive oil
Salt
Pepper

½ medium onion, minced
1 garlic clove, minced
1 garlic clove, peeled

1½ pounds/700 g clams,
   cleaned and scrubbed
2 pounds/1 k mussels,
   cleaned and scrubbed
4 ripe plum tomatoes,
   peeled and diced
8 slices country bread
10 basil leaves, torn
2 oregano sprigs, finely
   chopped

In a 3- or 4-quart/3- or 4-liter stockpot, cook the clams and mussels in the white wine until the shells open. Discard any shells that don't open. Strain the cooking juice through several layers of cheesecloth to remove sand. Set the strained juice aside. Remove half the mussels and clams from their shells; keep the other half in the shells to garnish the dish.

Sauté the onion and minced garlic in the olive oil until golden. Add the tomatoes and sauté for 1 minute. Add the shellfish juice and cook 10 minutes to reduce. Add all the clams and mussels. Season with salt and pepper to taste and simmer for 3 minutes.

Toast the bread and rub the crusts with the garlic clove. Lay the bread in the bottom of the serving bowl, ladle the soup and shellfish over it, sprinkle with the basil and oregano, and serve immediately.

SERVES 4

Mark:

Real *cacciucco* should be thick, more the texture of a stew made from everything that is left over. I used to make it with wine, tomatoes, and broth. Now I use lobster broth; it gives it a stronger, fishier taste with more body to it.

Marta:

I think that until about ten years ago it was much easier to find places where you could get *cacciucco* that was thicker and heavier. But in the last few years it is easier to find places that make a lighter soup with beans and artichokes and all the vegetables. It's like a new wave. It's good, but it is not really *cacciucco*.

When I was in Livorno I had a *cacciucco* at one of the most famous trattorias in Livorno. It was very thick, with a lot of essence of the shell.

You can eat *cacciucco* in a lot of places, and each one will be different. Everyone has a recipe based on the fish of the region and the cook's own individual taste, which may vary from city to city in the same region—maybe even from house to house.

The best *cacciucco* I ever had in my life was in a small restaurant called Luigi's, located in a house in Abruzzi where I stopped on my way from Calabria to Modena. The *cacciucco* was made with red and green peppers, fresh tomatoes, and lots of vegetables.

I still can't read what this guy wrote.

Mark:

Cacciucco can be very spicy when it's made with lots of pepper. The pepper acts like a cleanser, it makes your whole mouth alive.

Marta:

Usually it's spicier in the south. I've had very good, spicy *cacciucco* in Capri. The fish was cooked in a rich broth with fresh tomatoes and sea trout for just about ten minutes.

Mark:

For a really intense flavor I have used the broth that comes from the liquid we cook the heads and bones in.

Marta:

The problem in America is that most people don't want to see any bones. Maybe they eat half or three-quarters of the fish, but then if they see a bone they won't eat any more.

Mark:

I've discovered something being in the restaurant business in America. I don't think people know that fish have bones in them. Well, there really are bones in fish, and they come out of the sea, too.

G U A Z Z E T T O   D I   P E S C E   C O N V E R D U R E

L I G H T   S T E W   O F   F I S H   A N D V E G E T A B L E S

10 tablespoons / 150 ml olive oil

Pinch of crushed red pepper

½ cup / 125 ml white wine

Salt (optional)

2 garlic cloves, sliced

4 cups / 1 l fish broth (see page 91) or clam juice

2 carrots, julienned

2 celery stalks, julienned

2 potatoes, peeled, sliced, and blanched

1 garlic clove, peeled

Handful of minced parsley

32 clams, cleaned and scrubbed

16 mussels, cleaned and scrubbed

1 pound / 500 g monkfish, cut into small chunks

12 medium shrimp, peeled, with heads on

12 scallops

½ cup / 100 g fresh mushrooms, sliced

½ cup / 100 g fresh fava beans, skinned

1 small tomato, peeled and diced

4 slices country bread

In a large sauté pan, heat the olive oil over high heat, then add the clams and mussels. Cover and cook until the shells open, 4 to 5 minutes; discard any that don't open. Lower the heat, add the sliced garlic, crushed red pepper, and monkfish. Toss well. Sauté for 1 minute, then add the shrimp, scallops, and white wine. Taste for salt and add if desired. Cook until the wine reduces, then add the fish broth or clam juice. Bring to a boil, add the carrots, celery, and potatoes, cover, and boil gently for 5 minutes. Add the mushrooms, fava beans, and tomato. Remove from the heat, stir, and set aside for 5 minutes.

Toast the bread and rub the crusts with the whole garlic clove. Place a piece of bread in the bottom of each bowl and ladle in the soup. Garnish with parsley and a drizzle of olive oil.

S E R V E S 4

CHAPTER 8

One Public Mamma

PINO AND MARTA PULINI

The three lucky ones . . . roasted.

MARTA, MY EXECUTIVE CHEF AT LE MADRI, COMES FROM AN UPPER-MIDDLE-CLASS ITALIAN FAMILY. SHE HAS HAD A GREAT EDUCATION; SHE WAS MARRIED YOUNG; SHE HAD TWO CHILDREN AND FOR many years was a wealthy housewife. At one point in her life, she felt that she needed something of her own, something she had missed in the years she was raising her children. She decided to build a professional life from her experience as a cook. She brought to le Madri the technical expertise of a professional chef; she brought an approach to food rooted in her cultural background as a homemaker and cook. I've known many chefs, and often there's not much more to their experience than the time they've spent in cooking school. But I am fortunate to be surrounded by people who have interesting backgrounds and histories.

Marta had been on the restaurant scene for a couple of years before she and I sat down and talked about a collaboration at le Madri. Now she is the leading figure in the kitchen because of her commonsense approach to food and her unorthodox and creative way of running things and planning menus. She always leaves space for a certain amount of improvisation and encourages a more day-to-day approach to food, not a lot of planning but lots of spontaneity. That's the way it's done at home.

Marta is from Modena, near Valli di Comacchio, a swampland that is a natural reservoir for eels and many kinds of fish. I have fond memories of great meals in the area when I traveled there as an actor, and I love to share my memories of Comacchio meals with Marta. She connects with these memories because these are the dishes she grew up with and she remembers cooking as a young girl, a wife, a mother, and a chef.

A N G U I L L E   a l   R O S M A R I N O
E E L S   W I T H   R O S E M A R Y

Flour
¼ *cup / 60 ml olive oil*
¼ *cup / 60 ml balsamic vinegar*
½ *cup / 125 ml white wine*
Salt
Pepper

4 shallots, finely minced

*2 pounds / 1k eels,
cleaned, skinned, butter-
flied, and cut into
2-inch / 5-cm pieces*
1 large rosemary sprig

Roll the eel fillets into rounds and stick with toothpicks to hold them together. Dust in flour. In a sauté pan, cook the eel rounds in 3 tablespoons/45 ml of the olive oil until they are golden, about 4 minutes. Add the vinegar to the pan and cook until it has reduced slightly. Remove the eel, saving the pan juices. Set aside.

In a separate sauté pan, cook the shallots in 1 tablespoon/15 ml olive oil until golden. Add the white wine, rosemary, and reserved pan juices. Season with salt and pepper to taste, add the eels, and simmer gently for 2 to 3 minutes. Remove the rosemary, transfer the eels to plates, top with the sauce, and serve.

S E R V E S   4

IT'S ALWAYS NICE TO TALK to an Italian who has grown up in Italy; what I call a full Italian. The conversation is so easy, so immediate when we talk about the simplicity of regional dishes, the way things are thought out, constructed, presented, and sold.

There is a natural flow in the way I work with Marta. I think it's not only that we share a similar national outlook, but it's also that we share a similar outlook in the kitchen. Even though we are a certain number of years apart, she is closer to the thinking of my generation than people ten years younger than I am.

Marta was born before World War II, and I was born not long after, but Italy really didn't recover until the fifties and sixties, so significant generational differences weren't apparent until later. During the reconstruction period after the war, Italians identified themselves with certain values that had been established earlier: a certain morality, a certain ideology, a certain taste for life. After 1960 all that changed drastically. Marta and I can sit down and talk for hours about what our mothers taught us, what we were taught in school. From school we go on to our favorite Italian poets and from there to food. It is a natural progression for us.

M A R T A   T A L K I N G

A moment's respite.

"Modena is famous all over the world for its balsamic vinegar. It is very special because it is produced by individual families, not factories. You can find vinegar that is labeled "balsamic" for a few dollars, but real *balsamico* can cost more than a hundred dollars for just three ounces.

"Balsamic vinegar is not made from wine as are other vinegars; it is started from *mosto*—the skin, seeds, and pulp that are left over when the grapes are pressed for wine. The *mosto* is cooked outside in large vats over a wood fire in a process that originated in the fourteenth century, maybe even earlier.

"Unlike most vinegars—which require a constant, cool temperature during the aging process—*balsamico* needs extremes of climate. So it is placed in wooden barrels on the roofs of houses and exposed to the kind of weather common to Modena: hot and humid summers and very cold winters.

"If you could look over the roofs of Modena you would see on the top of almost every house a minimum of six barrels of diminishing size lying on their sides next to each other, each barrel supported by a hollowed-out slab of wood at each end to keep it from rolling. The barrels may be of many different kinds of wood—black chestnut, cherry, juniper, maple—it depends on the preference of the individual household.

"As the vinegar evaporates, it is moved to the next-smaller barrel. The longer it ages, the more precious it becomes, and some vinegars are left to age as long as fifty years.

"Because it isn't on the sea, Modena doesn't have a big tradition of fish, but we do have tripe fish for *zuppa di pesce,* or we fry or grill fish coming from the lake and the river. We have some eel and *cefalo,* a fish similar to the shad, and sweet-water fish like catfish or *luccio* and *cappa,* which is similar to perch. At one time there were a lot of sturgeon in the Po, but a few years ago the sturgeon disappeared. Now there are a lot of farm-raised sturgeon in the delta of the Po, where the water is very sweet."

R I S O T T O   C O N   P E S C E   G A T T O

R I S O T T O   W I T H   C A T F I S H

F O R   T H E   B R O T H

Salt

Juice of 1 lemon
1 celery stalk, cut into
    ½-inch / 1-cm pieces
1 carrot, cut into ½-inch /
    1-cm pieces
1 onion, halved
2 tablespoons / 32 g butter

2 pounds / 1k catfish
    fillets
1 scallion, finely minced

F O R   T H E   R I S O T T O

1½ cups / 285 g Arborio rice
¼ cup / 60 ml white wine
Salt
Pepper

6 tablespoons / 96 g butter
1 onion, quartered
10 cups / 12,5 l vegetable broth

To make the broth, put the lemon juice, celery, carrot, onion, and salt in a large stockpot. Add water to cover. Boil for 10 minutes. Reduce the heat slightly, add the catfish, and simmer gently for 5 to 7 minutes, or until the fish is firm. Remove the fish, break the fillets into chunks, and set aside in a covered dish.

Meanwhile, in a small sauté pan over high heat, sauté the scallion in 2 tablespoons/32 g of butter. Pour it over the catfish, cover, and set aside in a warm place.

To make the risotto, in a large saucepan over medium heat, sauté the quartered onion in 5 tablespoons/48 g of butter until soft. Add the rice and mix until the rice is coated. Add the wine slowly and reduce. Remove the onion. Add 1 cup/250 ml of the vegetable broth. Simmer, stirring occasionally, adding broth a little at a time until the rice is firm to the bite but not mushy. Season with salt and pepper to taste; add the catfish chunks and the remaining butter. Mix well and serve immediately.

S E R V E S   4

"F A T T Y   F I S H   M I X   W E L L with the balsamic vinegar from Modena. We use it to give a sweet-and-sour taste to eel, or we add a few drops on top of grilled fish or in salad. Each family has a particularly aged bottle that it keeps for a special meal or holiday, and one that is younger for marinating rabbit or chicken. The "balsamic" vinegars that are sold for a few dollars a liter may be used as a substitute, but it's not the same as the family-produced product."

Don't lose a drop.

FILETTI D'ANGUILLA CON ACETO BALSAMICO

FILLET OF EEL WITH BALSAMIC VINEGAR

½ cup/70 g semolina

1 teaspoon/4 g grated nutmeg

1 teaspoon/4 g ground
cinnamon

1 teaspoon/4 g white pepper

¼ cup/60 ml corn oil

Salt

4 tablespoons/60 ml olive oil

2 tablespoons/24 g golden
raisins, soaked

2 tablespoons/24 g pine nuts

Balsamic vinegar

2 pounds/1k eel, cleaned,
skinned, butterflied, and
cut into 2½-inch/6-cm
pieces

2 pounds/1k fresh spinach,
well cleaned

In a small bowl, mix together the semolina and the spices. Dip the eel into the semolina mixture until well coated and set aside. In a sauté pan, heat the corn oil and sauté the eel on both sides until golden brown. Drain on paper towels. Sprinkle lightly with salt. Set aside.

In a separate pan, heat the olive oil, add the spinach, and sauté until wilted. Add the raisins and pine nuts, toss lightly, and cook for another moment. Transfer to the center of a serving plate, ring with pieces of eel, sprinkle with balsamic vinegar to taste, and serve.

SERVES 4

"WHEN I WAS FIVE OR six years old my parents would take me by motorcycle from Milan to the beaches in Liguria almost every weekend. I would sit in the middle between my father in the front and my mother in the back, holding tightly to the basket which contained the family cat. We went to Portofino, Camogli, Punta Chiappa, which at that time were still real fishing villages, not crowded resorts like they are today.

"My mother and I would go out with my father in the early morning in a rowboat, and he would dive deep into the water with a speargun to fish. When we came back to our small hotel in the village, the cook would prepare whatever my father had caught. We had wonderful soups, whitebait or octopus fixed in many different ways. I remember these simple dishes with great pleasure."

T O R T I N O   D I   B I A N C H E T T I   E   P A T A T E
S M A L L   C A K E   O F   W H I T I N G   A N D   P O T A T O E S

¼ cup/60 ml olive oil
Salt
Pepper

2 medium potatoes
1 garlic clove, minced
1 teaspoon/4 g finely minced parsley

1 pound/500 g whiting, rinsed and drained
¼ teaspoon/1 g fresh thyme
¼ teaspoon/1 g fresh marjoram

Preheat the oven to 300°F/150°C. In a large stockpot, boil the potatoes in salted water until cooked but still firm. Drain and run them under cold water. Peel and refrigerate. When the potatoes are cold, slice them in ½-inch/1-cm slices.

In a bowl, mix the whiting, olive oil, garlic, herbs, salt, and pepper to taste.

Oil a baking dish and line it with a single layer of potato slices. Sprinkle with salt and pepper and place a spoonful of whiting mixture on each slice. Bake for 5 minutes, or until golden brown. Serve hot.

S E R V E S   6   A S   A N   A P P E T I Z E R   O R   4   A S   A   M A I N   C O U R S E

"A T   L O W   T I D E   I   W A T C H E D   the fishermen from the village on the beach looking for *tellina*, a shellfish similar to clams but much smaller and tastier. The fisherman carried large wooden poles with metal strainers on the bottom, which they used to pick up the *tellina*. They would drag the rake through the sand with a kind of backward hopping step, stopping to lift the strainer and toss the *tellina* into a bucket.

"The first time I went 'fishing' was for *tellina*. I would sit in the shallow water and stay for a long time playing. Using my hands as rakes, I made holes in the sand and searched with my fingers until I felt the hard little shells. I would rinse the *tellina* in the seawater, put them in a small bucket, and take them home where I helped my mother cook them in oil with garlic and a little white wine. I was very proud to have provided the food for our meal."

S P A G H E T T I   A L L E   V O N G O L E   I N   B I A N C O
S P A G H E T T I   W I T H   W H I T E   C L A M   S A U C E

Tellina are not readily available in the United States, but small clams, like Manila clams, work well as a substitute.

³/₄ *pound / 375 g spaghetti*
6 *tablespoons / 90 ml olive oil*
Pinch of crushed red pepper

1 *garlic clove, smashed*
2 *tablespoons / 24 g finely minced parsley*

2 *pounds / 1k Manila clams or other small clams, cleaned and scrubbed*

Cook the clams in a large sauté pan over high heat, using no oil. Discard any clams that do not open. Remove the clams from the pot, and remove most of the clams from their shells, keeping a few in the shell for garnish. Set the clams aside. Strain the juice released by the clams through several layers of cheesecloth to remove the sand and set aside.

Fill a stockpot with water. Bring to a boil and add salt. Add the spaghetti and cook until al dente. While the spaghetti is cooking, make the sauce.

In a separate pan, sauté the garlic in olive oil until golden. Remove the garlic and add the shelled clams and crushed red pepper. Sauté for 2 or 3 minutes, until they sizzle. Add the unshelled clams and half the reserved clam juice and cook 1 minute.

Drain the pasta. Add the spaghetti, parsley, and the rest of the clam juice to the clam mixture. If the sauce is too watery, add a little olive oil and a bit of butter and reduce quickly. Toss thoroughly and serve immediately.

S E R V E S   4

"M Y   Y O U N G E S T   S O N   A L S O   loves to go fishing. When he was small he sat on the shore of the river with a hook on the end of a line and waited for hours for a fish. He would come home every day with three or four small fish, and I would put them in the freezer to save for when he caught enough to make soup or pasta.

"Now he lives in Modena and usually he goes fishing in the river close to home. He also goes to Yugoslavia and Sardinia and spends hours waiting for the octopus hidden under the rocks, just like his father did years ago."

I N S A L A T A   D I   P O L P O   F R E D D O
O C T O P U S   S A L A D

3 bay leaves
Salt
Pepper
10 tablespoons / 150 ml olive
 oil

1 pound / 500 g potatoes
Juice of 1 lemon
2 tablespoons / 24 g finely
 minced parsley
1 garlic clove, finely minced

2 pounds / 1k octopus,
 cleaned and rinsed

Bring a large pot of water to a boil. Add the octopus, bay leaves, and salt and pepper to taste and boil gently for about 45 minutes, until the octopus is tender.

In a separate pot, boil the potatoes in their skins until they are cooked but still firm. Run under cold water, peel, cut into 1-inch/3-cm chunks, and set aside.

Drain the cooked octopus, cut it into 1-inch/3-cm chunks, and place in a large bowl. Drizzle with the olive oil and lemon juice; add salt and pepper to taste. Marinate for 10 minutes. Add the potatoes, parsley, and garlic. Mix gently and serve at room temperature.

SERVES 4 GENEROUSLY

"WHEN I WAS OLDER I liked to go to Porto Santo Stefano in Tuscany. I would take a knife, tuck a piece of lemon into the top of my swimsuit, and collect *padella* from the big rocks which line the coast. *Padella* is a shellfish which clings to the rocks by a suction pad almost like a single octopus tentacle. I would slip my knife between the pad and the rock and free the shell, squeeze lemon on the fish inside, and suck it out. I thought I was very refined because I used lemon. I lingered around those rocks for hours eating *padella*. They were so tasty and, of course, so fresh. They are not something that you can buy; you must go directly to the rocky beaches of Liguria or Tuscany and get them for yourself. I have never found them at the fish market.

"I like to look for *padella* even now. I am going to Sardinia soon, and I will take a knife and some lemon. I also like to gather my own small sea snails, although I don't eat them raw. I take them home and cook them.

"The summer that I was about eleven my cousin and I were staying with our grandmother at the beach on the Adriatic. We liked to walk on the docks in the harbor and watch the fishing boats return. Often the fishermen would be roasting their catch right on the boats, and they smelled so good cooking my cousin and I would look at them with hungry eyes. One day two fishermen took pity on us and invited us on their boat to have grilled fish. In Romagna it is traditional to bread the fish and grill it with garlic and rosemary. It was wonderful. We felt very grown-up, because our grandmother was not with us, and maybe we were showing off a bit, but we ate too much and by the time we got home I had a stomachache. I didn't want to tell my grandmother why because I felt sure she would be very upset that we had gotten on a boat with people we didn't know. My cousin and I still share that secret and the memory of that fish grilled on the boat."

ORATA ALLA GRIGLIA CON ERBE AROMATICHE
PORGIES GRILLED ON A BED OF HERBS

Marinate the whole fish for twenty-four hours before grilling.

4 tablespoons/60 ml
  vinegar
1 cup/250 ml olive oil
Salt
Pepper

Four 1-pound/500-g
  porgies or tilefish
4 rosemary sprigs
4 thyme sprigs
4 oregano sprigs
4 sage sprigs
4 marjoram sprigs

Place the fish in a dish with a large rim so you can cover them with the marinade. Mix the vinegar and olive oil together and pour them over the fish. Place the herbs on top, cover, and refrigerate.

Remove the fish and herbs from the marinade. Reserve the marinade. Wipe the excess off the fish and herbs so that it will not drip on the coals and cause the fire to flare up. Place the sprigs of herbs on the grill, then place the whole fish on top of the herbs. Cook for 5 minutes. Sprinkle with salt and pepper. Turn the fish over and cook about 5 more minutes. The fish is done when you pierce the flesh and a milky liquid runs out. Remove to a platter and fillet the fish. Sprinkle lightly with the reserved marinade and serve immediately.

SERVES 4

"MY HUSBAND OWNED A castle in Reggio Calabria on the top of a hill overlooking the little village of Calopezzati. Now he is my ex-husband, but he still owns the castle.

"Because my husband was a count, I was the countess. I never cared or thought much about this, although I knew that the people of the town observed the old traditions. One morning during the first summer that we moved into the castle I was picking up all the dead leaves and weeds in the garden, which had once been a moat around the castle, when a man came looking for the countess.

"I said, 'I don't know where she is, I don't think she's here.' I was embarrassed to be a countess in my sneakers and shorts, down there digging in the dirt.

"Frederick II built the castle in the thirteenth century when he was the king of Germany. He came down the boot of Italy on the way to Sicily by horseback, and for each day that they stopped along the way he built a castle to use as a way station. Starting from the mountains in Puglia all the way to the end of Calabria, the Ionic coast has a castle near the sea spaced the distance of one day's ride by horse.

"Life in this castle was outside of reality. All the country peasants from around the castle lived on the land and worked for my husband. They were farmers and fishermen. They fished at night in small boats with lamps to attract the fish, and every morning they brought us fresh fish, usually mackerel or sardines."

Small guys bathhouse.

S A R D E   I N   T O R T I E R A
S A R D I N E   T A R T

¾ cup / 143 g bread crumbs
¼ cup / 60 ml white wine
6 tablespoons / 90 ml olive oil
Salt
Pepper

3 ounces / 90 g Pecorino, grated
1 garlic clove, minced
2 tablespoons / 24 g finely
  minced parsley
3 eggs

2 pounds / 1k fresh
  sardines, cleaned and
  filleted

Preheat the oven to 300°F/150°C. In a bowl, mix together the bread crumbs, Pecorino cheese, garlic, and parsley.

Place a layer of the sardines in a 9-inch/23-cm springform pan. Pour all of the wine over the fish and sprinkle with some of the bread-crumb mixture. Repeat layers of sardines and crumbs until you reach the top of the pan, ending with a layer of bread crumbs. Drizzle with the olive oil.

In a separate bowl, beat the eggs lightly with salt and pepper to taste. Pour evenly over the sardines. Bake about 20 to 25 minutes, until a golden crust forms.

SERVES 6

"I REMEMBER VERY WELL my favorite fish, *aguglia*, which is like a very small swordfish, the size of a large sardine, but long and narrow, silver outside like a mackerel. *Aguglie* are very tasty but not too fat. We had a cook who made them into a stew with hot peppers and fresh Calabrian tomatoes ripened by the sun. I can't forget this, it was so good. We also had sardines breaded with herbs and put in the oven. These fish were so fresh you could still taste the sea. We had clams and mussels, which we made with just garlic, oil, parsley, very simple, served with bread croutons to soak up the juice."

A L I C I   F R I T T E
F R I E D   A N C H O V I E S

You can substitute fresh sardines in this recipe if anchovies are unavailable.

Flour
Bread crumbs
½ cup / 125 ml vegetable oil
Salt
Pepper

2 eggs
1 garlic clove, minced
3 tablespoons / 36 g minced
   parsley

2 pounds / 1k medium or
large fresh anchovies,
cleaned and filleted

Rinse and dry the anchovies. In a small bowl, beat the eggs with the garlic and parsley. Dredge the anchovies in flour and shake to remove the excess. Dip them into the egg mixture and then into the bread crumbs. Pour the oil into a sauté pan. Add more if it doesn't reach ¼ inch in the pan. Heat the oil until very hot. Add the anchovies and cook for 1 minute, turn, and cook for 30 seconds more, until golden. Remove them from the pan and drain them on paper towels. Sprinkle with salt and pepper to taste. Serve immediately.

S E R V E S   4

A L I C E T T E   M A R I N A T E
S M A L L   M A R I N A T E D   A N C H O V I E S

Salt
Crushed red pepper
½ cup / 125 ml extra virgin
   olive oil

Juice of 10 lemons
1 garlic clove, finely minced
2 tablespoons / 24 g finely
   chopped parsley

1½ pounds / 700 g small
fresh anchovies, cleaned,
heads removed, and
butterflied
3 tablespoons / 36 g finely
chopped fresh oregano

Lay the anchovies in a dish and cover with the lemon juice. Marinate for ½ hour, or until the meat turns white. Remove the anchovies from the lemon juice and lay them in a single layer on a large platter. Sprinkle with salt and crushed red pepper to taste, oregano, garlic, and parsley. Drizzle with the olive oil. Serve cold with tomatoes, cucumbers, toasted bread, and hard-cooked eggs.

SERVES 6

Look at those little guys.

"SOMETIMES WE WOULD GO to the docks when the big fishing boats came back, the ones that go three or four miles out from the coast. They would bring the tuna and the small, small anchovies, maybe one inch long and thin, thin, thin. The fishermen made me a present of these because they knew they were my favorite. The cook would just salt them, add a few herbs and hot red peppers, and put them in jars. Fish prepared this way is called *rosmarina*. My sons are going to the castle for vacation this year, and I am going to ask them to get the exact recipe for me. It is very spicy, and you can eat every part of it, as an appetizer or in a sandwich.

"The castle was about two thousand square meters and had a large terrace overlooking the sea. Inside were Aubusson carpets and a ballroom with a big fireplace. There were seven or eight bedrooms, big enough for my whole family: my husband, my two children, my father, my mother, my two sisters, and maybe one or two friends would come for July and August. We were a lot of people.

"We set up an open tent on the beach in the morning and stayed through lunch, which was brought to us by our *maggiordomo*, the butler, who had worked at the castle since he was fifteen, as had his father before him. He placed a table and chairs under the tent and opened a large cooler filled with good things: beautiful fish sandwiches, stuffed vegetables, rice croquettes. We would sit under the tent holding glasses of chilled white wine, cooled by the salty sea air, and listen to the waves crash against the Calabrian coast as we ate our lunch."

P A N I N O   a l l a   M A R T A

ANCHOVY AND ROASTED PEPPER SANDWICH

5 or 6 salted anchovies, rinsed
 and filleted
Olive oil

2 red or yellow bell
 peppers
Fresh oregano, chopped
1 large sourdough roll or
 ½ baguette

Roast the peppers by holding them on a large fork over the burner of a gas stove, turning until charred on all sides. You can also roast them under a broiler, turning to char on all sides. While the peppers are still hot, place them in a paper bag, fold the bag closed, and set them aside for about 20 minutes. When the peppers are cool enough to handle, remove the charred skin, taking care to remove all the little black specks. Core, seed, and cut them into ½-inch/1-cm strips.

Place the anchovies and peppers in a bowl, add oregano and olive oil to taste, and marinate for 2 hours in the refrigerator.

Split the bread lengthwise, spoon on the anchovies and peppers, close the sandwich, and serve.

SERVES 1

CHAPTER 9

Queens Story

PINO AND MARK STRAUSMAN

*B*EFORE I CHOOSE A CHEF, I TRY TO DIS-
COVER HOW HE OR SHE GREW UP, TO LEARN
WHAT CONNECTION THEY MIGHT HAVE HAD
WITH THE FOOD OF MY CHILDHOOD. I HAD
TO STRETCH MY IMAGINATION when I interviewed
Mark Strausman (who became the chef at Coco Pazzo) because the only
sardines he had ever seen came in a can. But I felt like his big heart
would be receptive to different tastes, to developing a new palate, knowl-
edge, and even affection for the underconsidered, small guys swimming
in the waters of these times.

I remember a conversation I had one afternoon with Mark. He and I
sat on the back patio of Sapore di mare and talked about what kind of a
future he hoped to have. I told him that I was the one taking the biggest
chance on him. I had hired a kid from Queens who wanted to turn into
an Italian chef. His previous experience consisted of four years as a chef
in hotels in Europe. He had worked in Holland, Switzerland, Germany,
and later New York. The food he knew was a combination of German
cuisine deviating into French with an American-Jewish inflection. I suggested he take all of that, throw it away, and I would turn him into a
trattoria type of cook specializing in Italian regional cuisine. He threw
himself into it completely.

I could see in Mark's face and tell by the things he said that he had
the emotions and heart of a true Italian chef. Even though he lacked
experience, I felt he really understood that for Italians food is more than
just eating. Today he is a super chef, and he keeps getting better. He has
been back and forth to Italy many times, eating and tasting.

Mark is a real success story. He puts up with a lot working with me
because I'm a tyrant in the kitchen, screaming and yelling and kicking,
and I don't let up until things are the way I want them. But my chefs and

Seasoning at Coco.

kitchen help stay with me. Probably because they know deep down inside they can go a long way with this guy. He's a nut, but he's fair. Either that or they need a job badly.

My staff and I gave Mark a new geographical identity. We redesigned the map of Queens, introducing more Italian names; we decided to make Mark from Florence Hill, on the Siena side of Queens, and we turned his name into Marco Uomostrano (Mark "Strange Man"). He had to endure a lot of kidding and joking about his ethnic background before he could blossom into an Italian protégé. He had many changes to make: through his mouth, his look, his understanding of what Italian food is really like. And he did it. He opened himself up to a totally different approach to buying, cooking, and selling food. He made a lot of mistakes at first, but his big heart prevailed, and more and more he came to resemble a big Italian mamma. He loves to be surrounded by food, drowning in food, overwhelmed by food. It looks like he's preparing for the end of the world.

Mark has researched ingredients used in Italian cooking, and he understands how they interact. He knows how to produce straightforward, simple, and spontaneous dishes that are the hallmark of Tuscan cuisine.

P A N I N I   A L L A   M A R K
M A R K ' S   S A N D W I C H E S

½ cup / 125 ml white wine
1 bay leaf
3 black peppercorns
Salt
Pepper

¼ medium carrot, cut into
  1-inch / 3-cm chunks
¼ medium onion, coarsely
  chopped
3 tablespoons / 45 ml
  mayonnaise
1 garlic clove, peeled
1 small red onion, thinly sliced

2 pounds / 1k whitefish
  fillets
2 scallions, thinly sliced
8 slices country bread
1 medium beefsteak
  tomato, sliced

In a shallow pan (or fish poacher, if you have one), bring ¼ cup/60 ml water plus the wine, carrot, chopped onion, bay leaf, and peppercorns to a boil. Lay in the whitefish, reduce the heat, cover, and simmer until the fish is cooked, about 10 minutes. Remove the fish, pat it dry, and set it aside to cool.

When the fish has reached room temperature, break it into chunks in a mixing bowl. Add the scallions, mayonnaise, and salt and pepper to taste and mix well, until the fish chunks are broken up and well coated with mayonnaise.

Toast the bread in the oven, toaster, or on the grill. Rub the crusts lightly with the garlic clove. Spread with the fish mixture, top with tomato and sliced red onion, and serve.

S E R V E S   4

P A N I N O   C O C O   P A Z Z O
O P E N - F A C E D   S A N D W I C H   C O C O   P A Z Z O

½ cup/125 ml white wine
2 tablespoons/30 ml red wine vinegar
½ cup/125 ml olive oil
Salt
Pepper

½ medium red onion, very finely minced
1 garlic clove, peeled

24 mussels, scrubbed
24 clams, scrubbed
½ red bell pepper, very finely minced
8 basil leaves, torn into strips
8 slices country bread

Place the mussels, clams, and wine in a large stockpot. Cook over high heat, stirring occasionally, until all the shells have opened, about 4 or 5 minutes. Remove the mussels and clams from the pan and discard any shells that have not opened. Remove all the shellfish from their shells and place them in a mixing bowl. Add the onion, red bell pepper, basil, vinegar, and olive oil. Mix well. Season to taste with salt and pepper and mix again.

Toast the bread in the oven. Rub the crusts with the garlic clove, pile each piece of bread with the seafood mixture, and serve immediately.

S E R V E S   4

M A R K   T A L K I N G

"My interest in fish goes back to my childhood. My father used to take me casting at Fort Totten, under the Throgs Neck Bridge. I don't remember ever catching anything, but I do remember buying fish at the docks. My brother and I loved to go down to the docks and wait for the boats to come in. We would watch the fishermen gut the fish and clean it for us to take home.

"My father died when I was fourteen, and later my stepfather and I would go fishing. My mother was not the most established cook in the world, but when she was cooking the fish we caught, she seemed to be having fun. There was a sparkle in her eye, and all of a sudden the scent of fresh lemons was in the house."

P E S C E   P I C C O L O   A L L A   G R I G L I A
S M A L L   G R I L L E D   B A B Y   F I S H

You can use any kind of small fish for this particular recipe. My favorites to use in the summer are black sea bass or farmed striped bass; in the winter I prefer brook trout. Other suggestions include whiting, grouper, tilefish, or porgies.

Salt
Pepper
¼ cup / 60 ml olive oil
2 tablespoons / 30 ml extra
   virgin olive oil

1 lemon, quartered
Juice of 1 lemon

Four 1-pound / 500-g
   small fish, cleaned and
   gutted
4 rosemary sprigs
4 oregano sprigs
4 tarragon sprigs
4 sage leaves

Fill the cavities of the 4 fish with a sprig of each of the herbs and a quarter of the lemon. Season with salt and pepper. Brush the ¼ cup/60 ml olive oil on the skins of the fish and place them on a red-hot grill. Turn the fish over once to cook evenly on both sides. Total cooking time should be about 10 to 12 minutes. Fillet the fish at the table and drizzle the lemon juice and extra virgin olive oil over the fish before serving.

S E R V E S   4

I do everything here.

"I GOT INTO PROFESSIONAL cooking when I was about twenty-one years old. I didn't enjoy my classes at Queens College, so I kind of finagled my way into hotel school in New York City. I enjoyed all my classes, but the cooking and wine classes suited me best.

"When I graduated, I got a job in West Germany for three months, but I ended up staying in Europe for four years. By now I knew for sure I wanted to be a chef. From Germany I went on to Switzerland for a year, then ended up in Amsterdam, where I was introduced to the glorious fish of the North Sea.

"I had been working at Il Cantinori for three or four months when Pino offered me a job at Sapore di mare. While I was there my enthusiasm for fish doubled and so did my ideas for preparing it. Then my wife and I spent two weeks of our honeymoon on the Tuscan coast between Viareggio and Grosseto and saw many of the same fish dishes that we were doing at Sapore. It gave me great confidence to know that what I was doing was authentic. I've been back to Italy many times since the Sapore days, and I am convinced that this cross-cultural exchange is much more challenging than just trying to create fanciful dishes out of my head.

"I've traveled in Italy from the coast to the mountains and have recently done research on the cuisine of Sicily. The Sicilians know so well how to mix fish with the nightshade vegetables—peppers, tomatoes, and eggplant. I picked up a typical regional fish couscous recipe in Sicily from the area near Marsala, which faces North Africa."

C U S C U S   A L L A   T R A P A N E S E

C O U S C O U S   W I T H   S E A F O O D , T R A P A N I - S T Y L E

F O R   T H E   F I S H   S T O C K

3 black peppercorns
1 bay leaf

1 carrot, chopped
1 celery stalk, cut into
    1-inch/3-cm pieces
1 onion, chopped
1 parsley sprig

1 pound/500 g fish
bones (flounder, sole,
and snapper work well)

F O R   T H E   C O U S C O U S

4 tablespoons/60 ml extra
    virgin olive oil
Pinch of crushed red pepper
Salt
Pepper
1 cup/250 ml white wine
1 box instant couscous

2 garlic cloves, sliced
1 onion, diced
1 carrot, diced
1 celery stalk, diced
Juice of 2 lemons
Chopped parsley

1½ pounds/700 g
    calamari
½ pound/250 g octopus,
    cleaned and cooked
12 mussels, cleaned and
    scrubbed
12 clams, cleaned and
    scrubbed
⅓ pound/166 g monk-
    fish, cut in 1-inch/
    3-cm pieces
⅓ pound/166g fresh cod,
    cut in 1-inch/3-cm
    pieces
1 pound/500 g whiting
    fillets

To make the fish stock place the fish bones, vegetables, peppercorns, and herbs in a stockpot. Cover with water and simmer for 45 minutes. Strain the stock through a very fine sieve and let it cool in the refrigerator.

To make the couscous place a large soup pot over medium heat and brown the garlic in the olive oil. Add the calamari, crushed red pepper, the vegetables, and salt and pepper to taste. Sauté until the vegetables are wilted. Add the octopus, mussels, clams, white wine, lemon juice, and ¾ cup/188 ml of the reserved fish stock.

Let the soup simmer slowly until the shellfish have opened and the broth has cooked well. Discard any shellfish that haven't opened. Then add the fish pieces and let the mixture simmer for about 1 minute, or until the fish is perfectly tender.

Make the couscous according to the package directions (you may use fish or chicken stock instead of water if you like a richer flavor).

To serve, place some hot couscous in each bowl and slowly pour the soup and fish around the grains. Garnish with chopped parsley to taste.

S E R V E S   4

Z U P P A   D I   C O Z Z E   E
V O N G O L E   A L L A   S I C I L I A N A
C L A M   A N D   M U S S E L   S O U P ,
S I C I L I A N - S T Y L E

F O R   T H E   S O U P

¼ cup/60 ml olive oil
1 cup/250 ml white wine
Pinch of crushed red pepper
Salt
Pepper

½ red onion, finely minced
2 garlic cloves, peeled

1 fennel bulb, sliced
3 ripe tomatoes, diced
30 clams
30 mussels
6 oregano sprigs

FOR THE GARLIC BREAD

1 tablespoon / 15 ml olive oil
1 teaspoon / 4g dried oregano

2 garlic cloves

8 slices country bread

In a large pot, sauté the onion, garlic, fennel, and tomatoes in the olive oil until wilted. Add the clams and mussels, white wine, crushed red pepper, oregano, and salt and pepper to taste. Cover and simmer until all the clams and mussels are open, about 5 minutes. Discard any shellfish that do not open. Taste the broth and adjust the seasonings.

To make the garlic bread, toast the bread and rub the garlic cloves over the bread. Sprinkle with the olive oil and dried oregano. Serve immediately.

SERVES 4

PASSERA DI MARE AL POMODORO E CAPPERI
FLOUNDER WITH A WARM SAUCE OF CAPERS, OLIVES, AND TOMATOES

FOR THE SAUCE

1 tablespoon / 12 g capers
4 tablespoons / 48 g black olives, pitted
¼ cup / 48 g sun-dried tomatoes
½ cup / 125 ml olive oil

2 tablespoons / 24 g chopped parsley

4 plum tomatoes, chopped

F O R   T H E   F L O U N D E R

Salt
Pepper
½ cup / 70 g flour
½ cup / 125 ml vegetable oil

1 lemon, sliced

Four ¾-pound / 375-g
    flounder fillets

Make the sauce by processing the capers, olives, sun-dried tomatoes, and parsley in a food processor until they are a rough puree. Mix the chopped tomatoes with the puree in a bowl. Slowly pour in the olive oil, mixing very well so it will emulsify. Set the sauce aside.

Season the flounder with salt and pepper, then dust with flour. In a large frying pan over medium heat, cook the flounder in the vegetable oil for 3 minutes. Turn the fish and cook it 3 minutes more. Both sides should be golden. Remove the fish from the pan and drain it on paper towels. Ladle a pool of the sauce on the serving plate. Place the fillets on top of the sauce. Garnish each fillet with a drizzle of extra virgin olive oil and a slice of lemon.

S E R V E S   4

IN NEW YORK CITY fish are dragged over pavement in cartons instead of being pulled out of the Mediterranean. But New York City is a great place to cook. If you're a competitive chef, one who's keeping up with trends and on the cutting edge, this is the best city in the world to be in.

"I try to prepare dishes that will make people aware that there are more fish in the sea than the prestigious tuna, snapper, salmon, and swordfish, which get so much of our attention. I like the words *frutti di mare*, 'fruit of the sea'; it means to me that the sea is full of beautiful fish that ought to be eaten."

I N S A L A T A   D I   M A R E
C O L D   S E A F O O D   S A L A D

2 tablespoons / 30 ml olive oil
1 cup / 250 ml white wine
Crushed red pepper
Salt
1 bay leaf
¼ cup / 60 ml extra virgin
   olive oil

1 garlic clove, crushed
½ celery stalk
8 parsley sprigs
Juice of 1 lemon

24 mussels, cleaned and
   scrubbed
24 clams, cleaned and
   scrubbed
1 pound / 500 g calamari,
   cleaned
½ pound / 250 g octopus
½ pound / 250 g scallops

In a sauté pan over medium heat, brown the garlic in the olive oil. When the garlic is golden brown, add the mussels, clams, white wine, and crushed red pepper to taste. Simmer until the shells have opened, about 4 or 5 minutes. Discard any shellfish that haven't opened. Remove the shellfish from the pan, saving the broth. When the shellfish have cooled, remove the seafood from the shells, and place it in a mixing bowl.

Cut the calamari into rings. Bring a pot of salted water to a boil and add the calamari rings and tentacles. Cook until tender, about 10 minutes. Remove the calamari from the water and cool.

Boil the whole octopus bodies in a large pot of water for about 30 minutes, or until tender. Remove the octopus from the water and cool. Cut the octopus into small pieces. Add the scallops and bay leaf to the reserved broth. Bring to a gentle boil and poach until the scallops are tender, about 3 minutes. Remove the scallops from the broth and cool.

Dice the celery and chop the parsley. Place them in the bowl with the shellfish. Sprinkle with a pinch of crushed red pepper. Add the juice of the lemon, 2 or 3 tablespoons of the juice from the seafood broth, and the extra virgin olive oil. Mix the salad well.

Check the seasonings, adding more oil if necessary. Serve at room temperature or warm. If you prefer the salad warm, simply heat it in a sauté pan.

S E R V E S   4

"YOU SHOULD ALWAYS buy the freshest fish possible. You can do many different things with all fish; fish are completely interchangeable. If you can't find red mullet to grill, I don't see why you can't grill baby perch just as well. It's not the same, but it will be good if it's fresh, I promise. When buying fish if you have to make a choice between the kind of fish and freshness, always choose freshness.

"If we were standing by the fishing docks and someone pulled in a whiting and offered me a simple pan-sautéed whiting at that moment or swordfish that came in a couple of days ago from Florida, I would have the whiting. There's nothing like the taste of fish right out of the water."

C A L A M A R I   P I C C A N T I
S P I C Y   S Q U I D

1/4 cup/60 ml extra virgin
  olive oil
2 tablespoons/24 g crushed
  red pepper
1/2 teaspoon/2 g dried oregano
Salt
Pepper

1 small red onion, finely
  minced
1 garlic clove, minced
Juice of 2 lemons
10 sprigs parsley, chopped

2 pounds/1k squid,
  cleaned
3 large plum tomatoes,
  cubed

Cut the squid into rings. Place the onion, garlic, and plum tomatoes in a mixing bowl. Place the squid in a large pot of boiling water and cook until tender, about 10 minutes. Drain the squid and add it to the onion-garlic-tomato mixture. Add the olive oil, lemon juice, crushed pepper, and herbs and toss well. You may serve this warm or at room temperature. Taste for salt and pepper.

S E R V E S   4   T O   6

PENNE AL TONNO IN SCATOLA

PENNE TOSSED WITH TUNA AND TOMATO

1 pound / 500 g penne
¼ cup / 60 ml extra virgin
  olive oil
¾ cup / 188 ml canned
  tomatoes
8 black olives, pitted
Salt
Pepper
Toasted bread crumbs

2 garlic cloves, peeled

One 6½-ounce / 195-g
  can tuna, drained
3 oregano sprigs

In a large stockpot, boil salted water to cook the pasta. Place the olive oil in a large frying pan over medium heat. When the oil is hot, add the garlic, tomatoes, black olives, tuna, oregano, and salt and pepper to taste, and allow the mixture to simmer until the tomato has cooked and thickened. Set aside. Cook the pasta until al dente, drain, and toss well with the sauce. Garnish with toasted bread crumbs and serve immediately.

SERVES 4

CHAPTER 10

Umbrella Fishing

PINO AND MASSIMO FIORILLO

WHEN I FIRST MET MASSIMO, HE WAS A
YOUNG KID IN HIS LATE TWENTIES WHO
WANTED TO MOVE OUT OF ITALY FOR A
WHILE AND WORK IN A DIFFERENT PART OF
THE WORLD. I THOUGHT IT WOULD BE AN
INTERESTING COLLABORATION.

Massimo comes from a family of restaurateurs; he was practically
born in a restaurant kitchen. He brings to Sapore his interpretation of
the authentic, family-run restaurant that is very common in Italy.

Massimo came into my life at the right time, at the right moment,
and proved to me one more time that the dishes he learned from his parents were the ones I would want in my restaurant. He started to work at
Sapore when I was beginning to run out of steam in my crusade to promote certain kinds of dishes and menus. In Massimo I found someone
who could recharge my efforts. In a cowardly way I intentionally didn't
warn him of the frustration he might come up against in trying to get
customers to accept certain dishes. It was rough for him the first two
months. He put so much love and attention into finding the right ingredients, cooking them with such great results, and presenting them with
grace, only to see a mediocre demand and response. He felt all sorts of
things that any chef would feel when he sees people not being receptive
and he knows he is doing the right thing.

We sat down to talk in the early summer when he had been at Sapore
for about two months. He said to me, "You know, it's hard for me to
understand what people want. I know I'm cooking real Italian food, and
every day a waiter comes into the kitchen bringing back food that has
been cooked perfectly and tells me that the customer says he doesn't like
it because it isn't Italian."

"Massimo," I said, "everything is subjective. You have one perception

Oops! I'm stuck with one extra.

of Italian food, and your customers have another. We are not here to educate; we are not a school of gastronomy; we are here to provide food the Italian way, and we will continue to do so. But first you have to establish a link between what the customer thinks is Italian and what really *is* Italian, or you're not going to be cooking for anybody. You have to think in terms of compromise, because that's the only way you'll achieve what you want. It's a slow process of introducing only one element at a time. For example, your beautiful mackerel that you make in the most beautiful, handsome way, I never had such mackerel or sardines or anchovies. Your sea robins are phenomenal. Or the way you make pasta with whiting, shad roe, and zucchini. You do incredible stuff. But our customers' palates did not develop the same way our palates developed, so you have to take the position that you know better, and knowing better you have to compromise. I suggest you offer five items: three are a perception of what the customer thinks is an Italian dish and two are for real. You have to introduce new things slowly, until you reach an understanding, and in no time the palate will develop and accept."

T A G L I O L I N I   A L L A   B O T T A R G A

T A G L I O L I N I   W I T H   S H A D   R O E   A N D   Z U C C H I N I

8 tablespoons / 120 ml olive oil
½ teaspoon / 2 g pepper
1 teaspoon / 4 g salt

Juice of ½ lemon
2 garlic cloves
¼ cup / 48 g chopped parsley

2 small shad roe (about ½ pound / 250 g), whole
1 pound / 500 g fresh tagliolini
2 medium zucchini, diced

To prepare the shad roe, gently remove the outer membrane, or sac. Hold the shad roe over a bowl and, with a cheesecloth, carefully brush the roe eggs into the bowl. Drizzle 1 teaspoon/5 ml of the lemon juice, 1 tablespoon/15 ml of the olive oil, and a pinch of the pepper over the eggs and set aside.

Bring a large pot of salted water to a boil for the pasta. When the water is boiling, add the fresh pasta.

Place a large sauté pan over medium heat. Sauté the garlic cloves in 6 tablespoons of olive oil until golden; add the zucchini and cook until they are soft, but not brown. Drain the cooked pasta in a colander and add it to the sauté pan. Lower the heat and add the parsley and the remaining pepper, tossing well. Remove the pan from the fire. Begin adding 1 tablespoon/12 g of the shad roe mixture and a small amount of the remaining lemon juice at a time, mixing well after each addition. Continue adding the shad roe and lemon juice until the sauce consistency is to your liking (the roe are rich, and some like more than others). Taste for salt.

When the sauce is the right consistency, place the pan back on medium heat. Quickly toss the pasta mixture about 5 times to mix the flavors. If necessary, add the remaining 1 tablespoon olive oil and toss. Serve immediately.

S E R V E S   4

I L   M A C H E T T O
S A R D I N E   P A T É

This is an old, traditional Ligurian preparation that is spread on toast or over pizza or tomatoes. In Liguria, it is also called anchovy paste, but it's really made with very small sardines.

Sea salt
Olive oil

Fresh sardines or anchovies, 2 to 3 inches / 5 to 8 cm long, cleaned, gutted, heads and tails removed

In a glass container, layer the fish, completely covering each layer with a generous amount of sea salt. Repeat until the jar is filled. Cover and set aside in a dark place to marinate (we call it *courcere*, "to cook") for 40 days. Make sure that you turn them every 2 to 3 days. When they are "cooked," press the salt-and-fish mixture through a very fine cheesecloth, making a sardine or an anchovy paste. Pack the paste in small jars, covering the top of the mixture with olive oil before sealing. Store in a cool place or the refrigerator. The mixture is very concentrated!

P **I** **Z** **Z** **A** **A** **L** **L** **A** **A** **N** **D** **R** **E** **A**
A N D R E A ' S   P I Z Z A

F O R   T H E   D O U G H

2 ounces/60 g dry yeast
8 cups/1k all-purpose flour
*½ cup/125 ml plus 2 table-
  spoons/30 ml olive oil*
1 teaspoon/4 g salt

1 cup/250 ml whole milk

F O R   T H E   S A U C E

¼ cup/60 ml olive oil
*10 anchovies, preserved in salt,
  filleted and rinsed*
*Two 1-pound/500-g cans
  Italian peeled tomatoes*
Salt
*4 tablespoons/48 g black
  Kalamata olives, pitted*

2 red onions, thinly sliced
*1 head garlic, cloves separated,
  skin on*

*1 teaspoon/4 g minced
fresh oregano*

Make the dough. Proof the yeast in ½ cup water. Pile the flour in a mound. Make a well in the center and pour in ½ cup plus 2 tablespoons/155 ml water, the milk, olive oil, yeast, and salt. Slowly and gently fold the flour to mix in the wet ingredients. The dough should be soft and stick to your hands. If it is too dry, add a little water. Do not overwork the dough. Spread the dough in a jellyroll pan, cover with a dish towel, and set it aside to rise until it doubles, about 1 hour.

Make the sauce while you are waiting for the dough to rise. In a sauté pan, cook the onions in the olive oil until golden. Add the anchovies, tomatoes, and salt to taste and cook for 20 to 25 minutes over medium heat. When the sauce has thickened, remove it from the heat and allow it to cool.

Preheat the oven to 300°F/150°C. Spread the sauce evenly over the dough, dot with garlic cloves at 1-to-2 inch intervals, and sprinkle with oregano and olives. Bake for 45 minutes, or until the crust is cooked through.

SERVES 6 TO 8

I TOOK A DEEP BREATH. "Massimo, you have to insinuate yourself into the peoples' minds, you can't attack violently; that creates problems, revolutions, wars. Once you believe in your strength and your knowledge, don't force it; introduce it slowly, gently, wisely."

Even though he agreed with me and he was willing to try a new tack, I knew it was rough on him. He was downhearted when he had to exchange sea robins and blowfish for tuna and swordfish.

I was watching him with affection, but I wasn't sad about his predicament; I was amused because he reminded me of myself. When he realized we were winning one battle at a time, his spirits picked up.

He started to relax and have some success with his dishes. Once he found a fisherman who had whiting, and he was so excited he bought all of them. I asked him how he intended to prepare that much whiting. "Oh, today I'm going to fry them. I'm going to flavor them with white wine vinegar and sage and serve them pickled. Tomorrow I'm going to make them into little cakes with egg yolks whipped in and a squeeze of lemon on top. But today I'll make a great whiting soup."

M I N E S T R A   D I   B I A N C H E T T I
W H I T I N G   S O U P

½ pound / 250 g angel-hair
  pasta
Salt
Pepper
2 tablespoons / 30 ml olive oil

4 cups / 1 l fish stock (see
  page 121) or you can substitute clam juice
Butter
1 large egg

3 large zucchini, diced
½ pound / 250 g whiting,
  rinsed

In a stockpot, blanch the zucchini in the fish stock for 3 minutes. Break the pasta into 1-inch/3-cm pieces, add it to the broth, and cook 3 minutes more. Add the whiting and cook it for 1 minute. Add enough butter to enrich the soup and season to taste with salt and pepper. Remove the soup from the heat and gently whip in the egg and olive oil. Serve the soup immediately.

S E R V E S   4

M A S S I M O   T A L K I N G

"My grandfather and my father were from Naples, and they were both fishermen. At night they went fishing, and in the morning they brought the fish back and sold it. They would place the fish in a small box filled with seawater to keep it alive until they returned to the harbor. My father learned all the important things he needed to know about fish from his father. It was their religion.

"My father worked with my grandfather in the fish market until he was eighteen and went into the navy. In the early fifties, he was sent to the small village of Imperia on the coast of Liguria near the French border where he met my mother, settled down, and where I was born.

"The knowledge of fishing that he brought with him was unusual for that area because the fishing techniques in the south of Italy—places like Sicily, Compania, or Sardinia—weren't yet known in the north. Liguria

had a very poor and simple fishing tradition, which was basically limited
to sardines, anchovies, mackerel, red mullet, octopus, and a few clams or
mussels that were caught near the coast."

F I N O C C H I   E   A C C I U G H E   S A L A T E
F E N N E L   A N D   A N C H O V I E S

1 tablespoon/12 g salted
 capers, rinsed and minced
12 anchovies, preserved in salt,
 rinsed
½ cup/125 ml olive oil
Bread crumbs

6 fennel bulbs, trimmed

Preheat the oven to 400°F/200°C. In a stockpot, bring water to a boil and cook the fennel
for 10 minutes. Drain, cool slightly, and slice it very thin. Oil a baking pan and line it with
the fennel slices. Top with capers and anchovies, drizzle with olive oil, and sprinkle generously with bread crumbs. Bake for 15 minutes, or until the top is golden.

S E R V E S   6

"THE FISHERMEN USED LONG nets that we call *sciabica*.
One boat leaves from the beach dragging the net as far as possible, heads
back, and then with maybe ten or fifteen people—men, women, and
children on each side—they start pulling the net toward the shore. All
the fish caught in the net on the trip back end up on the beach.

"Although I was born in Liguria, two-thirds of me is from the south,
so I learned from both the southern and northern traditions. My grandmother and my mother came to Imperia from a tiny village on the coast
of Sicily. They opened a small trattoria on the harbor, serving wine by

Massimo adds the final touch.

the glass and a few simple dishes from the south. They had been open for only a short time when my father was stationed at the navy building nearby. All the young sailors used to go to the trattoria for a beer and a plate of fried fish. That's where my father and mother met and started to have a feeling for each other.

"My father was a Neapolitan singer. He still is. Before the restaurant really got started he went with a small orchestra to the big hotels and cafés in Alassio and San Remo and sang all through the night for American and English tourists. The name of my parents' restaurant is Lanterna Blu, which comes from a very popular melody of those years.

"My father invested his singing money back into the restaurant for new chairs, new tables, new glasses, and a lot of seafood to cook in the simple southern Italian way, unknown to the Ligurian people."

Liguria is a very narrow strip of land squeezed between the sea and the mountains, and the Ligurian cuisine is a very simple one. The profile of Liguria is one of terraced fields built in small steps, of cultivated land that the farmers have stolen from the stones and rocks of the mountains. This method of terracing to grow food was borrowed from the Benedictine monks in France. This is a very hard land to grow things on, and that is why the Ligurians have a reputation for being very frugal.

"Ligurians grow and use lots of herbs like basil, parsley, mint, and rosemary. Marjoram is one of the most important and frequently used herbs. We are very proud of our marjoram. For the Ligurian people it is one of the most noble and important ingredients."

S A R D I N E   A L   F O R N O
B A K E D   S A R D I N E S

This dish can be served hot as a main course, but it also makes an excellent cold sand-wich filling with lettuce and a good country bread.

Bread crumbs
Olive oil
Salt
Pepper

2 garlic cloves, thinly sliced
Pinch of minced parsley

2 tomatoes
1 pound / 500 g fresh
   sardines, cleaned and
   heads off
1 tablespoon / 12 g minced
   fresh oregano
Pinch of minced fresh
   majoram

Preheat the oven to 400°F/200°C. Blanch the tomatoes in boiling water to loosen the skins. Peel, seed, and cut the tomatoes into cubes; set them aside. Oil a baking pan and line the bottom with the sardines. Top with the garlic, tomatoes, and herbs, sprinkle generously with the bread crumbs, and drizzle with olive oil. Season to taste with salt and pepper. Bake for about 20 minutes, or until the sardines are firm and the tops are golden.

S E R V E S   4

"I WAS PRACTICALLY born in my parents' restaurant; my mother had to run to the hospital in the middle of cooking dinner! From the time I was a very little child, I was always in the kitchen or the dining room, so I learned a lot about restaurants. I started by doing small jobs, serving plates, bringing wine bottles and bread to the tables. Each day I arranged a beautiful, big display of seven or eight baskets of seafood just in front of the restaurant for the customers to admire as they came in.

"When I was only five years old, I started fishing with my father at night with a harpoon and a light to attract the fish. In the early after-noon, I went with him to the fish market, and when we returned to the restaurant, I stacked the fish in the refrigerator and checked them for freshness every day. I learned how to open and clean oysters, mussels, and clams. I had to make sure they were very clean because we had a lot of customers who enjoyed eating them raw with lemon. I would spend every feast weekend just opening shells all day. I would prepare maybe two, three, four hundred shellfish.

When I was older I used to go to the beach to look for a particular kind of sea urchin or rocky crab we call *gritte pelose*. I would bring them back to the restaurant for my mother to cook in the shell with garlic, capers, black olives, and fresh tomatoes. I think they are much tastier than lobster."

S P A G H E T T I   C O N   R I C C I   D I   M A R E
S P A G H E T T I   W I T H   S E A   U R C H I N S

If you are lucky enough to find fresh sea urchins, grab them. Once you find them, you have it made, because this is a very simple recipe. If you don't know how to clean sea urchins, buy them already cleaned. Then enjoy this pasta, which has all the flavor of the Mediterranean in it.

One 12-ounce/360-g box no.
  11 spaghettini
2 tablespoons/30 ml olive oil
¼ cup/60 ml white wine
1 teaspoon/4 g crushed red
  pepper

Juice of 1 lemon
4 garlic cloves, smashed
2 tablespoons/24 g coarsely
  chopped parsley

16 to 20 sea urchins

With a teaspoon, extract all the orangy-red roe of the sea urchins. Sprinkle with the lemon juice and set aside.

In a large stockpot, boil water for the pasta. When the water is boiling, add salt, then the pasta. While the pasta is cooking, make the sauce. In a sauté pan, cook the garlic in the olive oil until golden. Add the white wine and reduce. When the pasta is al dente, drain it, and add it to the sauté pan. Sprinkle with crushed red pepper and parsley and toss well until all the pasta is cooked. Plate the pasta in equal portions on 4 plates. Top each with equal amounts of sea urchin roe.

S E R V E S 4

"I DEVELOPED A SYSTEM for catching crab all by hand. I would spear a small fish on the end of a stick, which I carried in one hand, and in the other I had a piece of string with a slipknot. I lured them out of the rocks with the fish, and when they came out of hiding I would tighten the slipknot around them and drop them into a basket. It would take me all afternoon to cover a half mile and collect twenty or twenty-five crabs.

"On another day I would crawl along the rocky beach moving the stones, looking for eels. I carried an old ruined fork to use as a harpoon, or I would just wrap a towel around my hand and try to grab them when they poked out of the rocks. Another way I caught eels was with a large open umbrella in one hand and a piece of cord bound around a big bunch of large worms (we call them *lombrichi*) in the other. I would hold the worms over the water, and then wait. The eels are crazy for these worms; it's their favorite bite. As soon as I felt an eel grab the worms, I pulled up the cord and shook it into the umbrella. If I had a successful day, the specialty that night would be fried or grilled eel."

A N G U I L L E   A L L A   S A L V I A
B A B Y   E E L S   I N   S A G E

The tiny eels you want for this dish are available from Spain, Portugal, and Italy in January, February, and March. They are expensive but extremely delicious. They are also known as baby sandy eels and blind eels.

½ cup / 125 ml olive oil

Salt

Pepper

2 garlic cloves, mashed

Zest of ½ lemon

6 or 7 fresh sage leaves

½ pound / 250 g baby
  eels, cleaned, rinsed,
  and drained

In a sauté pan, cook the garlic and sage in the olive oil until golden. Add the eels, stir quickly, cover, and cook over high heat for 5 minutes. Remove the lid, season with salt and pepper to taste, and cook for a few more minutes to reduce the liquid. When a white foam emerges from the eels, they are cooked. Drain off the olive oil, sprinkle the eels with lemon zest, and serve very hot.

S E R V E S   4

"FISHING WAS AN INEXPENSIVE way to spend time, because even if you didn't get any fish you also didn't spend any money. You didn't have to buy hooks; you didn't have to buy bait; you didn't buy anything. You just brought your old umbrella and a piece of cord and came back with a suntan. Of course, the next day you had to go to the fish market.

"The fishing boats came back between two and three in the afternoon. They brought the fish to the market a couple of miles from the restaurant, where they were sold to the restaurants and fish shops at auction. Imagine an enormous scale and three or four hundred cases of fish that were only a few hours old. 'Look, we have ten pounds of beautiful red mullet. I want fifteen dollars a pound. Thirteen? It's not enough.

Fourteen? Fifteen? OK, it's yours.' Fish that fresh is expensive—if you have to buy it.

"I always went fishing with my grandfather when I visited him in Naples. My grandfather had great respect for fish, and he taught me a lot about the traditions surrounding food and what food means to Neapolitans.

"There is an event from my childhood that I will never forget. My grandfather was well known among the fishermen of Naples. When he died, the funeral procession passed through the street where he had supplied so many people with seafood; all the houses closed their shutters to show respect. But the most moving moment came when we passed in front of the fish market where my grandfather had worked for so many years of his life. As the casket approached the storefront, the owner came out to where all the cases of fish were set out for display and covered them with towels. Even the fish gave a last *saluto* to a serious and honest fisherman.

"When I was growing up, the Ligurian culture of seafood was based on the coastal fish, particularly anchovies, sardines, and the babies of both, which we call *bianchetti*. We get the *bianchetti* from anchovies in the summer and in the winter from the sardines. They are delicious little fish, only about an inch and a half long.

"There is also in Liguria a very ancient and typical recipe made with mackerel—poached mackerel with sautéed onions and green peas, a touch of fresh herbs, such as marjoram, and a drop of extra virgin olive oil when it's ready on the plate. But a more modern Ligurian dish is mackerel which has been marinated and grilled with vegetables."

Cooking is easy.

MERLUZZO E VEGETALI ALLA GRIGLIA

MARINATED MACKEREL WITH GRILLED VEGETABLES

If you don't have a grill, the marinated fish and vegetables can also be baked in the oven.

Salt

Pepper

Pinch of crushed red pepper
  (optional)

¼ cup/60 ml extra virgin
  olive oil

2 tablespoons/30 ml balsamic
  vinegar

Vegetable oil

2 garlic cloves, sliced

Juice of 1 lemon

Six ½-pound/250-g
  Spanish mackerel fillets

1 rosemary sprig

1 oregano sprig

1 thyme sprig

1 eggplant

1 fennel bulb

1 large zucchini

Fresh oregano

Lay the fish fillets in a bowl. Sprinkle them with salt and pepper to taste, and crushed red pepper if desired. Dot with the garlic and herbs. Pour the lemon juice, extra virgin olive oil, and balsamic vinegar over the fillets. Place them in the refrigerator to marinate for 24 hours or overnight.

Slice the eggplant into ½-inch/1-cm rounds. Place the slices on a plate, sprinkle them with salt, and let them sit for 3 hours so that the bitter juices will be released. Drain the eggplant and set it aside. Slice the fennel lengthwise about 1¼ inches/3 cm thick. Try to keep the pieces whole for grilling. Cut the zucchini into ½-inch/1-cm strips. Season all the vegetables with salt and pepper to taste, and brush them with vegetable oil.

To grill the vegetables, place the zucchini on the grill first. After 1 minute, place the rest of the vegetables on the grill. After vegetable pieces have been on the grill for about 1 minute, rotate them about 45 degrees to give them "X" marks. Grill for another minute or so. Turn and grill on the other side, rotating again for the "X" marks. When the vegetables are cooked through, remove them from the grill and set them aside on a platter. Before serving (they are also tasty at room temperature), drizzle them lightly with extra virgin olive oil and sprinkle them with fresh oregano.

Remove the fillets from the marinade, wiping off the excess oil so it will not drip into the grill. Lay the fillets on the grill and rotate them after a minute or two to make the "X" marks. Cook for a few minutes more, until cooked through. Serve the fish on platters with the vegetables. If desired, heat some of the fish marinade in a sauté pan until the garlic and onion turn brown and sprinkle it over the fish before serving.

S E R V E S 6

"LIGURIA IS A REGION so parsimonious in its way of life and shopping habits that it offers a good example of how to organize a daily meal with very little money. Even now, although I work in a first-class restaurant in America, I still make seafood the way I was taught by my parents. I try to cook the modest fish, as well as the noble fish, as simply as possible, so as not to lose the special flavor and taste of that particular fish.

"We do a lot with canned and salted food in Liguria—salted anchovies, salted and preserved mackerel, air-dried tuna, canned tuna. This is an important step in the coastal seafood tradition. Preserve it when there is too much, and keep it for the long winter. When anchovies are cheap, spend a couple of days canning them. Every summer when I was a kid we bought one hundred to two hundred pounds of anchovies and put them in glass jars—a layer of fish, a layer of salt, a layer of fish, a layer of salt, and so on, put a weight on top, and let it all set. About six weeks later we washed off the salt and ate the anchovies in a salad, on a sandwich, on a pizza, or in a pasta."

T O R T A   D I   A C C I U G H E

A N C H O V Y   P I E

You can use fresh or salt-preserved anchovies here. The salted ones should be rinsed before preparation.

F O R   T H E   D O U G H

3 cups / 420 g all-purpose flour
6 tablespoons / 90 ml olive oil
Salt

F O R   T H E   F I L L I N G

¼ cup / 60 ml olive oil
3 cups white bread crumbs
Salt
Pepper

2 garlic cloves, minced
½ cup / 125 ml milk
4 tablespoons / 48 g grated
  Parmesan cheese
3 large eggs
1 tablespoon / 16 g butter

1 pound / 500 g Swiss
chard, cleaned and cut
into strips
1 pound / 500 g fresh
anchovies, cleaned

To make the dough, knead the flour with the olive oil, salt, and a little warm water—just enough to make a smooth, soft, shiny dough. Pat into a ball, cover with a light dish towel, and set aside.

Make the filling. In a large sauté pan, cook the garlic in the olive oil until golden. Add the milk, Parmesan, eggs, bread crumbs, butter, and salt and pepper to taste. Mix well. Add the Swiss chard and mix again.

Preheat the oven to 375°F/190°C.

Divide the dough into 2 pieces, one slightly bigger than the other. On a floured board, roll out the bigger piece until it's very thin and large enough to cover the bottom and sides of an 8-inch/20-cm round pan with deep sides. Oil the pan. Lay the dough in the pan, forming the dough up the sides, overlapping the top by ¼ inch. Spread a layer of the Swiss chard mixture on the bottom, then a layer of anchovies, and continue to layer until you reach the top of the pan.

Roll out the other half of the dough and lay it on top of the pie, pinching the top and bottom pieces together all around. Perforate the top in several places so the steam will escape as the pie is cooking. Brush with olive oil and bake for 40 minutes, or until golden. This pie can be served either hot or cold.

S E R V E S   4

A C C I U G H E   S O T T O   S A L E
A N C H O V I E S   P R E S E R V E D   I N   S A L T

This recipe is for people who can find fresh anchovies but can't find anchovies preserved in salt at the market.

Sea salt

Fresh anchovies, heads removed

Lay the anchovies in 1 layer in a large nonreactive baking pan. Cover with rock sea salt and let them sit for 24 hours. This will take away all the blood from the anchovies and make them stiff. In a large cylindrical glass jar, place 1 layer of anchovies facing in the same direction with their bellies down in the bottom of the jar. Cover with a layer of sea salt. Place another layer of anchovies on top of the first, with the tails facing in the opposite direction. Cover with a layer of sea salt. Repeat the process, each time laying the fish belly down, but facing a different direction from the previous layer. End the top layer with sea salt. Place a 3-pound/1,5-k weight on top of the salt, and cover the jar. Refrigerate for 1 month.

Over a period of time, the salt will create a salty liquid, which we call *salamoia*. This liquid will overflow the lip of the jar, so be sure to place the jar in a container to catch the *salamoia*. Save the *salamoia* in the refrigerator, emptying the container about once a week.

After a month, remove the weight and pour the reserved *salamoia* back into the jar, as it helps to preserve the anchovies longer. The *salamoia* becomes progressively clearer over the month, so use the clearer liquid first, adding as much of the older *salamoia* as needed to fill the jar.

"EVERY SUMMER IN Liguria we also preserved tuna by rolling fillets in a blend of salt and black pepper and then hanging them in the kitchen window for a couple of months to dry. We call this *mosciame.*"

LA CONSERVA DI TONNO
TUNA CONSERVE

1 quart / 1 l white wine vinegar
1½ pounds / 700 g coarse salt
Whole black peppercorns
Bay leaves

Twelve 5- to 6-ounce /
150- to 180-g tuna
steaks, 1½ inches / 4 cm
thick

Bring 1 gallon / 4 l of water, the vinegar, and salt to a boil. Reduce the heat, add the tuna, and simmer for 1 hour and 15 minutes. Drain into a colander lined with cheesecloth and cool. When the tuna is cool, place it in a covered container and refrigerate it for 24 hours.

The next day, sterilize four 1-quart / 1-l canning jars in boiling water. When the jars are cool, put the tuna in the jars and top each with a few peppercorns and a layer of bay leaves. Cover the jars tightly and place them in a stockpot of boiling water. Process for 45 minutes. Make sure to put a layer of cheesecloth at the bottom of the stockpot to keep the jars from breaking. Remove from the heat and let the jars cool in the water. Set the jars of tuna aside for at least 2 months so the tuna has time to tenderize. You have to wait, but it's worth it. If you find the abdominal part of the tuna—the dark part—you're in luck. It is a delicacy and is delicious served on bread as a sandwich or cold as an appetizer.

MAKES 4 QUARTS

"STOCCAFISSO, A DRIED CODFISH, has a long tradition in the Ligurian cuisine, as does *baccalà,* the salted codfish. It is easy to make. First you salt it for at least one week, then you boil it for fifteen to twenty minutes, take the skin off and the bones out, and the meat is ready to be cooked any way you want."

B A C C A L À   I N   U M I D O
C O D   W I T H   T O M A T O   A N D   B A S I L

F O R   T H E   S A U C E

2 tablespoons/30 ml olive oil
Salt
Pepper

Juice of 2 lemons

6 plum tomatoes
4 scallions
12 basil leaves

F O R   T H E   F I S H

¾ cup/188 ml white wine
3 black peppercorns
Salt
Bay leaf

1 onion, chopped
½ carrot, chopped
1 celery stalk, chopped

Four ½-pound/2,25 k
fresh cod fillets

Make the sauce. Cut the tomatoes into ¼-inch/0.5-cm cubes. Slice the scallions as thin as possible. Clean and dry the basil and tear the leaves by hand.

In a small bowl, mix the tomatoes, scallions, basil, lemon juice, and olive oil. Toss well. Season with salt and pepper to taste. Set the sauce aside.

To make the fish, in a braising pot place the white wine, ¾ cup/188 ml water, peppercorns, salt, bay leaf, onion, carrot, and celery. Bring to a boil. Add the cod and let the mixture simmer lightly until done, about 10 minutes.

Remove the cod from the liquid and place it on a platter. At this point, you can chill the fish or serve it. Either way, spoon some sauce over it before serving.

S E R V E S   4

"THE PILLARS OF THE Ligurian gastronomical culture are extra virgin olive oil, fresh vegetables, and fresh seafood. In the sixties doctors made a study to find out why people in the south of Italy, especially on the coast, are so healthy, why their level of cholesterol and incidents of heart attacks are so low. The results showed that is because they are eating fresh seafood, simple vegetables, legumes, carbohydrates, minerals, and extra virgin olive oil instead of animal fats."

S A R D I N E   A R R O T O L A T E
R O L L E D   F R E S H   S A R D I N E S

1 tablespoon / 12 g pine nuts
1 tablespoon / 12 g raisins
2 cups / 380 g bread crumbs
2 tablespoons / 24 g sugar
2 tablespoons / 30 ml red wine
  vinegar
½ cup / 125 ml olive oil
Salt
Pepper
Bay leaf

1 medium red onion, thinly
  sliced

2 medium fresh tomatoes
Pinch of fresh dill
1 pound / 500 g fresh
  sardines, cleaned, filleted,
  and butterflied

Preheat the oven to 350°F/180°C.

Blanch the tomatoes in boiling water to loosen the skin. Cool, peel, and chop very fine. Chop the pine nuts, raisins, and dill together. Toast the bread crumbs in a sauté pan until golden. Add the sugar, vinegar, oil, tomatoes, pine nuts, raisins, dill, and salt and pepper to taste. Cook, stirring well, until the mixture heats through.

Oil a large baking dish. Spread a generous layer of the bread-crumb mixture onto each fish fillet. Roll up the sardines and lay them in the baking dish. Stick a bay leaf and a slice of onion between the rolls. Bake for 20 minutes and serve immediately.

S E R V E S   4

"I T   I S   A   V E R Y   H A R D and long process to try to change people's eating habits. Let's hope they will learn through this book because they need to know about these fish for their home budget. They could save a lot of what they are paying for fish now just by knowing a little more about inexpensive seafood such as sandy eels, squid, grouper, porgies, whiting, whitebait, sardines, anchovies, and mackerel. For a few dollars you can make a delicious meal from these fish."

C A L A M A R E T T I   I N   P A D E L L A
P A N - S A U T É E D   B A B Y   S Q U I D

If you ever come across baby squid at the fish market, buy them. Have them cleaned and bring them home to give yourself one of the purest and most wonderful dishes you could possibly have.

3 to 4 tablespoons / 45 to 60 ml olive oil
2 tablespoons / 30 ml balsamic vinegar
Salt
Pepper

2 garlic cloves, smashed
1 tablespoon / 12 g chopped parsley

1 rosemary sprig, leaves picked
1 to 1½ pounds / 500 to 700 g baby squid or cuttlefish, cleaned

In a sauté pan, heat the olive oil and sauté the garlic and rosemary until the garlic is golden. Add the squid or cuttlefish a little at a time so the oil doesn't cool down too much. After 2 to 3 minutes, as they start to sizzle and stick to the pan, splash with vinegar and sprinkle with salt, pepper, and parsley.

Cook a little longer to let the vinegar evaporate. The squid are cooked when they begin to stick to the bottom of the pan again. If you are using larger calamari, cook slightly longer, until they turn white. Serve immediately.

S E R V E S   4

"I AM TRYING HERE and in Italy to stop the snobbish habit of serving and eating the most expensive fish. My purpose is to persuade at least some of our readers to go into a fish shop, look at the fish, look at the price, buy the three or four cheapest kind of fish, go home, and cook it in any of the ways that we suggest in this book."

I N S A L A T A   D I   R I N F O R Z O
S A L A D   O F   S T R E N G T H

4 tablespoons/48 g black
  Kalamata olives, pitted
6 anchovies, preserved in salt,
  rinsed and halved
1 tablespoon/12 g capers,
  rinsed
¼ cup/60 ml olive oil
2 tablespoons/30 ml red wine
  vinegar or balsamic vinegar
Salt

2 red or yellow bell
  peppers
1½ pounds/700 g
  cauliflower

Roast the peppers by holding them on a large fork over the burner of a gas stove, turning until charred on all sides. Place the peppers in a paper bag, fold to close, and let them sit for about 20 minutes. When they are cool enough to handle, remove the charred skin, taking care to remove all the little black specs. Core, seed, and cut them into strips.

Clean the cauliflower and separate it into small florets. Blanch it lightly in boiling salted water until al dente. Do not overcook—the florets should still have a little bite to them. Drain the cauliflower and then run it under cold water to stop the cooking process.

Place the olives in a large bowl. Add the anchovies, peppers, cauliflower, and capers. Drizzle with olive oil and mix gently until everything is coated with oil. Add the vinegar 1 teaspoon/5 ml at a time to taste. Season to taste with salt. This may be served at room temperature or chilled.

S E R V E S   4

INDEX